A GUIDE TO CREATING WEALTH PROCESSES, GETTING
FINANCIAL RESULTS, AND TRANSFORMING YOUR LIFE

Secrets to

BREAKTHROUGH

Wealth

PAUL KINDZIA

CPA, MBA, CFP®

Secrets to Breakthrough Wealth

A Guide To Creating Wealth Processes, Getting Financial Results, and Transforming Your Life

Copyright © 2016 by Paul Kindzia, Inc.

www.paulkindzia.com

ISBN: 978-0-692-70876-7

Published by Paul Kindzia, Inc.

Printed in the United States of America

Cover Design – Thomas McGee

Editing – Cathie Ericson, Angela Kindzia, Paul Kindzia

For other queries, contact:

questions@paulkindzia.com

Disclosures

By reading this book you recognize that this is for education purposes and there are no guarantees for specific financial results. By law, we cannot guarantee your specific results. So you agree to not hold us liable for any results, good or bad, that you get from our informational and education content. You alone are responsible for your outcomes in life.

We do not believe in get rich schemes or overnight success programs. We believe in hard work, adding value, servicing others, processes, learning, adapting, and overcoming obstacles that stand in our way between where we are in life and what our goals are.

Please note that nothing within these pages, on any of our websites, videos, or any content or curriculum is a promise or guarantee of specific individual results. We cannot offer any legal, medical, tax, or investment advice on an individual case by case basis within this content. Any financial numbers referenced are illustrative of concepts only and should not be considered average results, exact results, or promises for actual or future performance.

Paul Kindzia, Inc. is not a registered investment advisor and thus cannot give investment advice on an individual or case-by-case basis.

Making financial decisions based on any information presented should be done only with the knowledge that you could experience significant losses. Use caution and seek the advice of qualified professionals when attempting any lifestyle change, business opportunity, or financial endeavor. Check with your own accountant, lawyer, or professional advisor before acting on any information.

This concludes with all of the regular legal mumbo jumbo, disclosures, and disclaimers. We look forward to serving you with the highest standard of integrity and transparency. We value the trust that you put forth with us.

For additional valuable information including free resources, please visit our website at:

www.paulkindzia.com

Most people never build adequate wealth which leads to daily stress. We teach proven financial processes based on timeless principles that results in happier, more fulfilling, and balanced lives. We laugh a lot too.

ACKNOWLEDGEMENTS

Thank you to my family. It's one thing to repeatedly state, proclaim, yell, shout, preach, and grandstand that your most important investment is in yourself, your body, and your health. It's another to walk the walk and arrange one's affairs to live that philosophy yourself day after day. It would be impossible to eat, sleep, exercise, rest, recharge, push myself, learn, work, read, observe, travel, consult, write, produce, and get through the days without the unending support that it takes to fuel the machine. I am so fortunate and grateful for my family, "the pit crew" that keeps me on the race track loop after loop running full throttle. And when I bump the track walls or crash into others you bring me into the shop, bang out the dents, and apply a little polish with spit shine along with abundant elbow grease. Thank you. I love you tons!

To Dave and Renee, things are LooKin' good with a capital K. I learned more than I thought at DHT. Thanks for the push.

"The hardest part of writing a book, is reading a hundred. But it's also my favorite part." **– Paul Kindzia**

TABLE OF CONTENTS

How My Quest For Wealth Began

Have you ever wondered if your wealth levels are progressing at the right speed?

Have you ever felt that you were not progressing as fast as you should in regards to your financial situation?

Have you ever felt stuck at a certain level of wealth and wondered how to breakthrough to a higher level?

Have you ever wondered what common denominators of success exist in other wealth builders?

Hi. My name is Paul, and I'm a wealth builder. In fact, I'm a lot like you in that I wanted to transform myself financially and live a better life for myself.

Like all wealth builders, I had to start somewhere, and truth be told, I often wish that I didn't have to start so far back towards the end of the line compared to others. Perhaps you feel this way as well. Many times I wish I could do it even faster and I bet you wish you could too.

Where I Started

When I started my wealth building journey, I struggled severely. I had little financial resources, little knowledge, and I lacked access to mentors. What I lacked in resources, I made up for in ambition. I had a strong desire to make financial improvements in my life even though I had little idea of what I was doing.

Even with a strong level of ambition and commitment, that didn't mean I was always confident in what I was doing. Nor did that ambition ensure that I was taking the most effective or efficient steps to improve my situation in the least amount of time. It was safe to say that I encountered many problems along the way and each step along the journey brought new obstacles to overcome.

I consider myself the ultimate do-it-yourselfer, possibly to a fault. But many times I didn't know any better because I didn't know another way and didn't have people who could help me earlier in my journey. Therefore, I tried and worked hard to figure everything out myself. In the end, that served me well as I learned not to rely on people who perhaps I should not trust in the first place.

I strived to learn financial concepts to a fanatical level and for that reason, I'm pretty sure I went through more obstacles and pursued more fruitless directions than you will want to go through yourself.

When I was a kid growing up, our family didn't have much money. My father was a union electrician and worked commercial construction which often entailed dirty jobs within industrial facilities and chemical plants.

My mother stayed at home and took care of me and my five siblings, four sisters and a younger brother.

There were eight of us living in the house and we had to share a single bathroom. One learns the meaning of patience when sharing a bathroom with five women living in the same house.

We also owned a fishing and tackle store in the basement of our house to generate extra income. Yes, we were the family who sold worms, leeches, and crabs so you can just imagine the comments that I would get on the school bus. But because I loved fishing, I believed that having a fishing store was like owning a candy store. At that time of my life, I hated school and was not a gifted student. Instead I preferred getting off the school bus, grabbing a fishing pole and heading to the river, which was much easier when I had access to all the bait and tackle that a kid could carry.

"Accounting" For My Career

After high school, I obtained an accounting degree, figuring that was a good place to start if I wanted to learn about business, money, and wealth since accounting is the language of money, which I firmly believe to this day.

But I wasn't done yet. Somewhere along the line I had learned to enjoy school after all. I was genuinely interested in business and the opportunity to learn about specific topics while in college was refreshing. After undergraduate school, I pursued an MBA in corporate finance, which built upon the number-crunching skills I'd honed in undergraduate school.

I joined the honors accounting fraternity, Beta Alpha Psi during my college education years and eventually became the treasurer and then president of our honors fraternity chapter at the State University of New York at Buffalo.

You could say that I was the official president of the honors accounting geeks. Head honcho right in the thick of the number nerds, front and center. Looking back, it's hard to believe I didn't get many dates in college, what with my bait and tackle background and a title like that on my business card!

After completing graduate school, I landed my "dream job" in 1994 as a CPA and auditor at Ernst & Young, the large, global accounting, auditing and consulting financial services firm. They allowed me to pick an office to work out of anywhere in the United States to begin my career, and I chose Atlanta.

Now mind you, I had never even visited Atlanta before my interview with the firm, but I knew I wanted to get out of the cold of Niagara Falls, N.Y. which is right on the Canadian border. The 1996 Summer Olympics were set in which seemed cool and the economy seemed to be doing far better than it was in Buffalo, N.Y., which was the largest nearby city and therefore had been my best hope for landing a "real job" after graduate school.

If you couldn't find a job in Buffalo or Rochester, then the back-up plan was to go to New York City. At the time, I thought New York City was only where crazy people lived which was the general impression of most people who lived in upstate New York. But my world was admittedly rather small. My grandparents made a point never to leave the county unless it was essential, and most people I knew never left the neighborhood for any reason.

Aggravated in Atlanta

So you could say that everything seemed to be going right for me, except for a few small problems. First, I hated my job. But I was afraid to tell anybody because of my excitement about landing this "dream job." This was the job that every accounting student targets coming out of college.

Why did I hate my dream job you ask? Have you ever worked in Corporate America? If so, extrapolate all of your common experiences of working in a stuffy environment with a power hierarchy above you and then multiply that by a factor of five. It was a case of a square peg being forced into a round hole. I didn't go to a fancy private school, play golf, or know which fork to use at a client dinner. The politics were being played about four levels above my core competencies.

The second problem was that my relatively small salary made it very difficult to live in a large metropolitan city, even if at the time Atlanta had a relatively low cost of living. I had an apartment payment, student loans, a car loan, credit card loans, and all the typical living expenses. Fortunately my childhood prepared me adequately to live on Mac N' Cheese and canned soup while my paycheck went to things like parking fees and dry cleaning in downtown Atlanta.

Creating a Firm Foundation

I earned the required on the job experience to obtain my CPA license and eventually quit the firm, hung up a shingle, and started my own tax and accounting firm.

Over the years, I was able to build up a steady clientele and began adding supplementary services, such as financial planning and wealth management. You could say I had to learn along the way because that's always been my approach. I would figure out the essentials as I needed them as best I could. Clients would come to me with questions or problems and if I didn't know the answer, I would do the required research and reading to come up with the best possible solutions to address their needs.

As an avid reader, I gobbled up books, magazines or any resource that I thought would help me in my quest to "figure out how to become wealthy." I still have that habit, in fact, I worked hard for what I strongly desired, and that was an opportunity to become wealthy in my own lifetime.

The goal in my financial practice was to discover how to accumulate wealth for myself in addition to helping others who wanted similar goals. I figured that if I could watch and observe others who were successful, that would be tremendously valuable as well.

In that way, my firm became a big ongoing experiment and laboratory as it allowed me to see what goes on behind the front doors and curtains of households. I was shocked as to what I discovered. Spoiler alert! What you see is not what you get as far as the actual amount of wealth of the people that pretend to be wealthy.

I took notes and started tracking common denominators of success and failures. I searched for consistencies and similarities amongst those I wanted to emulate.

Becoming Your Guide

Over the years, I learned a lot of lessons on money and wealth. Now, after well over two decades worth of experience, I'm at a much different place than I was when I started out. Along the way, there were many financial concepts I learned and acquired that can help any aspiring wealth builder. I hope to guide you through some of those concepts as you progress on your own journey.

Maybe you are just starting out and don't know what to do. That's common. When most of us start out, we don't know many other wealth builders whom we can learn from. Fortunately there are specific steps and action items that I can help you focus on.

Maybe you have mastered a few financial concepts but want to progress to a higher level. There is always a higher level of wealth that is attainable.

I can relate to all of those questions and uncertainties. There is a tremendous amount of knowledge to learn, and it's hard to sort through much of the noise. If you feel stuck where you are, I can relate to that as well. There were plenty of times that I found myself stuck at a certain level of wealth, income, or lifestyle, and had to figure out how to get out of that phase and navigate around an obstacle. I'm still learning how to climb to higher levels and I'm still discovering new tricks, techniques, tools, and tactics to get me there.

The learning and journey will not stop; it will simply evolve because the world never stops changing.

As much as I am a "do-it-yourself-er," I still needed plenty of other people to help me along the way.

I needed books written by those eager to share their knowledge and experience. I needed the magazines and online articles. I needed and found value in blogs of people whose journey I found interesting and similar. I needed and found plenty of additional learning courses.

And now I feel obligated to distill what I've learned and pass on what I've learned (and where I've failed) to others who also want to build wealth.

Writing is something that I love, but in an odd way it often feels strange for writers to share their thoughts and knowledge. Writers all have that fear. Who am I to share opinions and knowledge with others? Who will listen? What if people don't like what I have to say?

I've felt those fears myself. But I also realize how thankful I was for others who took the time to write out their thoughts and experiences, and in that same spirit, I believe that there are those who will find my words helpful to them.

If you have fears, doubts, confusion, or wonder if you could move up the financial ladder, I can tell you with certainty that it is possible. It doesn't matter where you came from or where you started. The rules of money are universal.

That's not to say that acquiring wealth is easy. It's not. But for some, the journey is better than the alternatives. My preferred saying is, "The juice is worth the squeeze."

When times get hard, when you get tired, when you have failures, when you feel alone and missing out on other experiences, have faith. Although there is a certain amount of randomness to many parts of life, you can control far more than you realize.

Periodically it is important to take the time to observe and acknowledge what happens if you don't take care of yourself financially. Nobody else is going to do it for you. So many people find themselves without adequate financial resources in the later stages of life. The only thing in their pockets is a list of regrets. One of those regrets is usually, "I wish that I had not been so stupid and wasteful with my money."

There is a huge downside to negligence. Do yourself a big favor: Acknowledge it. Accept it. Run from it.

In any case, I hope you find the following nuggets helpful on your path to wealth success and a happier and more fulfilling life. Please note, there is no way to teach over 25 years' worth of experience in a short 200 page paperback book. That would be an impossible task.

This book is a compilation of short chapters that highlight many of the issues you are likely to encounter along your journey. Successful wealth builders execute these fundamentals repeatedly. These are the foundations to success. Many may even appear to be common sense. Common sense often does not mean common practice.

The chapters are assembled in a particular order that you may find helpful as you proceed through the book. Depending on where you are along your journey, your life experiences, and wealth history, not every topic or chapter may resonate with you at this moment. But it is likely that you will eventually progress through all of these issues and items on your own individual and personal timeline in life. When that time comes, I hope you will refer back to this book time and time again.

The information in this book is not formatted as a textbook based upon theoretical knowledge. Nor is the information an encyclopedia of complex and technical jargon that confuses people. The book is a compilation of very practical and useful approaches to the action items that actually matter when it comes to wealth building. The objective is for others to make improvements in their life through better personal financial management without having to go through all of the heartaches and frustrations that I had to navigate. It's not necessary to become a CPA or certified financial planner or obtain advanced degrees in finance to improve your life. The statistics back that up. You can do it and I hope this book helps you along your journey.

Instructions Not Included At Birth

Have you ever wanted something so badly that you can feel your body and muscles getting tense just thinking about it? That's how it can feel with wealth building for many individuals. It is frustrating to want something so badly in life but not have the tools, resources, or knowledge to get there. Wealth is something that many people want desperately, yet it seems to elude the vast majority of the population.

Earlier in our lives and careers, that is often our situation. You want something tremendously, but you feel like you are stuck in the middle of a giant life riddle without the answers. Confusion results in a high amount of pain and frustration. It is the source of angst, turmoil, and teeth-grinding migraine headaches.

Where To Turn?

What most wealth builders discover in regards to self-made wealth building is that, "instructions are not included at birth." Or at least, you won't find them from the traditional sources of information, like family, friends, and public education institutions. In fact, wealth building is a puzzle and a riddle. The answers are always right there in front of you, but you can't pick them out. Wealth building revolves around a lot of common sense, but unfortunately applying common sense is surprisingly uncommon in real-world situations. Humans are a flawed species with many behavioral issues and quirks.

What is often the most frustrating to wealth builders is the speed of the process (or lack thereof), as it seems to take longer than most people prefer. If you're like most, you probably want to be wealthy RIGHT NOW. Information is great, but what about the results and transformation? That is what you are after. You want the fast solution that will change your life from frustration to contentment.

Feeling Your Pain

Wealth builders often experience a significant amount of internal pain which is the result of wanting an increased level of financial resources, and having a genuine desire to go after it, but then running into various obstacles that stem from the issue of "what to do now?"

Wealth builders aren't content just sitting on the couch and watching TV hoping that their lives will mysteriously and miraculously change. Real wealth builders are willing to make the efforts to change the course of their lives, and pursue the struggle from one obstacle to the next. Although they struggle, they consistently evolve.

As President Clinton once said, "I feel your pain." Although you don't know if he did or didn't feel your pain, if you are an aspiring wealth builder seeking to move to higher levels of wealth, then there is no doubt about the pain that you feel.

This book is assembled with your pain and struggles in mind and the knowledge that will be required for you to progress. As you triumph over the pains and obstacles, you will generate incremental results. They will not always be smooth, but they should occur based on your skills at implementing the foundations and proven processes of wealth building. Over time, these incremental results will continuously transform you as an individual.

You will not always see or feel this transformation happening in your life. But others will. It's similar to being a parent. You won't see the daily changes as your child grows up but periodically others will proclaim, "Oh my, little Joey is growing up fast!"

Building Your Foundation

In this book, you will learn about the many obstacles that you will encounter as a self-made wealth builder. You will learn what core knowledge is needed to progress continuously throughout life so that you AUTOMATICALLY do the important behaviors and processes every day, every week, every month, and every year of your journey.

You will learn how to execute on the fundamentals of wealth building, and you will improve your efficiencies and have more energy. You will connect with fellow wealth builders and people who can assist you. You will learn what to look out for and identify key success factors in different personalities. You will find yourself discovering opportunities to increase your income and set up your life situation so that you don't get distracted by losing money or by using ineffective methods that will cost you valuable time.

As you grow your wealth based on solid fundamentals and proven principles of success, you will grow in all areas of your life. Steady progress will lead to more satisfaction and fulfillment even if the journey is challenging and hard.

Developing Habits That Lead To Success

If you learn the foundations of success described in the following chapters, you'll avoid a lot of mistakes, hold on to more of your hard-earned capital, and save precious time, all of which will allow you to grow your wealth at a faster and steadier rate.

Most individuals fail at wealth building because they lack the necessary core behaviors. They also lack correct processes. Most individuals or households will never achieve wealth levels that are in line with their individual desires. Statistics back this fact up. Look at those around you in your communities and take note of how few people are living with financial freedom. There are reasons why there are traffic jams on Monday mornings as everybody is driving to work.

The best way to make sure you do the important processes every day is to make sure that your habits and behaviors are consistent with those that lead to wealth success. Once your habits and behaviors are consistent with those that lead to success, you don't have to think about it so constantly or get distracted by too many decisions. Making choices and decisions will become much easier as they will be made automatically and by default.

It turns out that you perform the same routines each day because you are a creature of habit. You go through the same steps day after day. The trick to wealth building is to figure out how to do the items that LEAD to wealth building instead of doing those that keep you stuck in your ways or keep you wherever you are in life.

Steps To Success

Here is your action plan to get yourself to perform the important wealth-building processes every day so that you can make incremental improvements with your finances, continuously gain the knowledge you need to progress, and increase your upper limits of potential;

1. Become a lifelong learner. Education doesn't stop with high school or college; in fact, they are just the beginning. High school and college do not do adequate jobs of giving you the information on what is truly important in life, namely health, wealth, and happiness.
2. Live each day based on principles of success. When you have proven principles to follow, you no longer find yourself aimlessly wasting your days wondering why progress isn't happening. We will discuss specific principles of wealth in an upcoming chapter.

3. Don't get distracted and stay diligent. You can't do all
    the right processes and behaviors on Monday through
    Friday to then revert to poor habits on the weekends and
    expect long-term success. Wealth building is a lifelong
    journey that requires a constant commitment to the core
    essence of the chosen path. It could only take one poor
    choice to derail years of hard work.

Start Now

The best time to start taking action in your life is RIGHT NOW.
If you want the benefits of being at a higher level of wealth then
you must start doing what it takes to get the information that
you need, attract the people who can help, and obtain the
financial resources that it takes to get to that higher level.

You will find that writing important items down has multiple
benefits. Begin by writing down important ideas and thoughts
that you generate on increasing your income, habits that you
need to create to improve your savings, and principles that you
want to follow with spending and investing. Write these down
in specific detail.

If you are going to start saving money, write down how much
you are going to start saving, how you are going to do it, and
where you are going to store those savings. Clarify and be
specific on how much you will save daily, weekly, or monthly.
Mentally visualize you earning income and saving the desired
portion.

The more specific you can be, the higher the benefit during your execution. If you are trying to save more, be specific as to how much you will save in your 401k, your emergency fund, and your brokerage account. Determine how much debt you want to pay down and eliminate. Be specific.

Imagine the steps that are required to create new habits and behaviors. These habits and behaviors will pave the way to your path of wealth. You must discover what processes have to be developed and implemented, and then take action on those processes.

Put actions and to-do's on your calendar, your phone, and your journals. Make processes automatic, such as scheduled savings using auto-draft. Remind yourself each day what it is you are seeking to do – BUILD YOUR WEALH.

Just because your life started with "instructions not included," doesn't mean that you can't obtain everything necessary to achieve your desired goals. You just need to assemble some individualized sets of instruction based on what you want to achieve. This book is designed to serve as the resource on your core instructions that you need for wealth success.

What's A Breakthrough?

break • through

noun

- A sudden, dramatic, and important discovery that leads to a large advancement or development in success resulting in a powerful transformation in personal wealth accumulation.

During your wealth journey, it is your goal to seek out and achieve as many breakthroughs as possible in as short of time frame as reasonable.

Wealth accumulation is not and will not be achieved in pure linear fashion. Life is never a straight path to any destination. Life is full of ups and downs, triumphs, and failures along with plenty of periods of stagnation or personal plateaus.

Many people also have very distorted expectations on wealth building or how most people accomplish financial goals. They often expect success to be an event that takes place where one is anointed and is accepted into the club with all the benefits of financial freedom. Rather than a step by step and cumulative progression, they want to believe that success kicks in overnight in one-fell swoop resulting in immediate transformation from poor to rich.

If we were to draw out and chart the wealth growth expectations of many individuals, it would look like this:

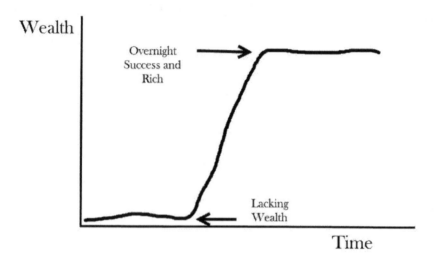

But we know that wealth isn't an overnight event. Success is earned over much longer periods of time. Thus, it could be quite useful to study those who have accomplished wealth success and seek out the common denominators of success.

One necessary and common denominator of success amongst wealth accumulators is their ability to bust out of periods of stagnation and plateaus and experience what can be described as "breakthroughs." These breakthroughs are those moments in your life where knowledge, experience, and action all come together in a way that elevates you to a higher level of personal achievement.

Breakthroughs require effort. Breakthroughs require persistence. Breakthroughs require patience. But breakthroughs are the difference between success and failure and transforming your life. Without them, you will end up like the majority of people who constantly spin their wheels but make no forward progress in life and are only left to wonder, "Why am I not succeeding?"

If we were to draw out breakthroughs on a sheet of paper, they would look like this:

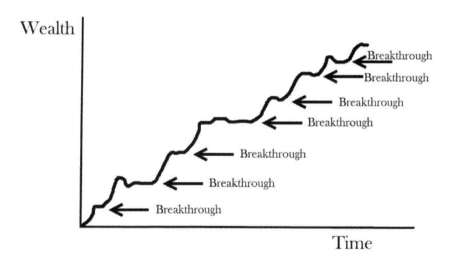

Breakthroughs are those moments where you bust through a period of stagnation or coming off a personal plateau where forward progress has slowed to a grinding halt. Plateaus are a natural part of life.

Part of mastery is practice and repetition and we could never master anything without practice and repetition. But how would you be able to master anything if you spent all of your time trying new things and constantly implementing change? You would never be able to master anything if you never spent the necessary time practicing the fundamentals that were required with that stage of your personal development.

This is no different in any craft or activity. It applies to art, basketball, playing the piano, or learning math. Progress is never linear because you have to spend ample time mastering certain skills before more advanced skills could be added to your repertoire.

This book is about laying out the foundations of wealth building in a way that when comprehended and implemented will lead to breakthroughs. These breakthroughs are what will transform your life. It won't always be easy. Some breakthroughs will take more time than others. But if you apply yourself and submerse yourself in the lifestyle, you will get positive results.

In Search Of Wealth

There was a man who built his significant wealth through real estate. There was a woman who built her significant wealth as a technology consultant. Someone else built wealth as a dentist.

You are searching for and desire to pursue a better path to wealth. You are searching for your unique and magical financial achievement, a destination where you think you will no longer have a care in the world. You want to be financially safe and comfortable. Happy. Proud. Accomplished. Respected. Wealth builders need to know that their hard work made an impact on life. The impact is not only on their life but on others' as well.

You may have already discovered that you want more wealth than what you currently have. Why is it that many can't agree on how to build and acquire it? Some say that it is just a numbers game. Others say it is about pursuing a passion. Many argue it is about hard work and sacrifice. Is there a right way? Is there a wrong way?

There are many paths to wealth. You must discover your unique and personalized path that is based on your personality, priorities, and core skills.

How Process Expedites Wealth

The very best wealth builders execute personal practices that are far more effective than those of most individuals. One area of expertise that wealth builders possess is in the area that can be described as "process." When you think of the term "process," I recommend that you imagine the word "software."

Software and Process Development

Software programmers write code based on a sequence of instructions that should be executed. For software to work properly, all steps necessary to complete the task must be included, and the instructions have to be in the correct sequence.

Wealth builders organize their life around personal sets of instructions that become so engrained in their daily behaviors that they perform those tasks automatically without much thought. It is similar to a person brushing their teeth each night before heading to bed. You do this automatically without having to write yourself a "to-do" reminder note or follow a written set of instructions. You subconsciously and automatically brush your teeth in a certain way, moving your brush in a similar pattern and similar time duration each night. You don't brush your teeth for 20 minutes one night and then 30 seconds the following evening. Nor do you subconsciously move your brush in a new direction or start in a different place one night from the next. You have built a process over time, and you execute the process repeatedly.

Wealth builders execute processes based on 7 fundamental principles of wealth success. These 7 fundamentals will be repeated in various places throughout this book. It is imperative that you learn and ultimately master these 7 principles of success. They are:

1. Generating Income
2. Controlling Spending
3. Saving Capital
4. Eliminating Debt
5. Building and Maintaining Adequate Emergency Funds
6. Managing Investments
7. Using Prudent Risk Management In All Areas Of Your Life

Wealth builders focus on specific objectives that encompass 1 of the 7 areas listed above. They move from one area to the next, balancing them out in a way that maximizes their wealth accumulation.

Imagine for a moment that you had a goal of getting in better physical condition to improve your state of health. To reach your objective, you will have to build processes and accomplish tasks specific to your desired outcome.

You might determine that the action that could most greatly help you in becoming healthier would include exercise, nutrition, sleep, and stress reduction.

Becoming healthier now must include the building of processes (writing the software) that helps you complete daily tasks that are in line with your desired results.

Developing Processes To Help You Commit

Let's start with exercise. You would begin by brainstorming different ways that you could complete more physical activities during the week. Examples might include:

- Lifting weights at a gym
- Swimming on your lunch break
- Going for a walk with your spouse

Let's take the first example – lifting weights at a gym. What are the actual physical steps required to make this happen in your day? They would include the specific tasks of:

1. Putting workout clothes in a gym bag
2. Putting the gym bag in your car
3. Driving your car to the gym
4. Walking from the car to the gym, into the locker room, and changing clothes
5. Getting on the workout floor
6. Executing a workout routine
7. Heading back to the locker room to shower and change
8. Exiting the gym

You may be reading this and be saying, "Duh, this is so basic and simple. How is this going to build my wealth and give me the results that I desire?"

The difference between those that achieve wealth and those that are left only with hopes and dreams is that achievers execute the software each and every day. They complete every step, in the proper sequence. They follow their individualized written instructions of tasks that need to be completed to achieve results. They don't ask themselves how they feel and use feelings to dictate their actions. They don't wonder what else they could do that is more fun or relaxing. They don't imagine being at home watching television while eating a bag of chips. They don't get distracted daily by doing non-essential tasks that waste precious time. Rather, they run the software each and every day on the items that relate to their wealth-building pursuits.

Success stems from developing personal software and then running that critical software each and every day in pursuit of the objectives that are your priorities.

Have you ever met a marathon runner or an Ironman Triathlete? Do you think each and every day the marathoner wakes up early and says, "I totally feel like getting out of this warm bed and going out in the cold weather and completing my training (running the software)?" That is not reality. Marathoners, athletes, professionals are all human. They like relaxing and resting as well as the next person. The difference is that they don't behave based on how they feel at any particular moment of the day. Rather, they behave and run the software required at that time of day to accomplish their necessary tasks.

At mile 18 of the marathon when their legs start to seize up, ache and hurt, the marathoner doesn't stop running and say, "My legs hurt. I want to go home and rest and eat pizza." Well, maybe they do but I'm sure they quickly trump those distracting thoughts and they say to themselves, "You have a task and objective to complete. Run the software in its entirety (which includes crossing the finish line and obtaining the finishers medal)." They complete all tasks in the proper sequence and then move on to the next required task (which may include eating pizza AFTER they accomplish their required tasks and objectives.)

Successful wealth builders are no different. They create processes that evolve as time progresses to help them reach higher levels using the 7 principles of wealth:

1. Generating Income
2. Controlling Spending
3. Saving Capital
4. Eliminating Debt
5. Building and Maintaining Adequate Emergency Funds
6. Managing Investments
7. Using Prudent Risk Management In All Areas Of Your Life

Our job as wealth builders is to build and execute personal software each day that moves us towards our desired objectives.

Applying Processes to Wealth Building

You can take any of these 7 principles and start building software that is necessary for achievement. If you want to generate more income, you need to begin by brainstorming different ways that appeal to you. Would it be to start a small company on the side? Would it be to get promoted? Would it be to change careers and find something that pays a higher wage? Once you determine what it is you need to do (the "What" and the "Why") then you need to write the software that tells you the proper sequence of tasks to complete (the "How.")

It's not that successful people don't have human feelings. The difference between wealth builders and non-wealth builders is that they run daily software that ensures they are doing the critical items necessary for success. They don't get hung up on how they feel at any particular moment throughout the day. The emphasis is on the doing, not the feeling.

High achievers base their day on a high number of personal software programs that have been refined over time as they acquire more skills and become more efficient, thus making them able to handle more complex tasks. The evolution of personal progress is required and applies to any skilled application, not just to wealth building.

The magic starts to happen when you begin running software easily, efficiently, and without thinking about the specific tasks. Say you want to save money each month, and you determine you want to put 10% of your gross monthly income into a taxable brokerage account. An efficient wealth builder takes the steps to set up an automatic monthly withdrawal from their checking account into their taxable brokerage account for the proper amount.

The software now is automated. You don't have to think about it. It doesn't matter how you feel on the 15th of each month when the auto-transfer occurs. It doesn't matter if you are tired, worked late, have the flu, or your child has a baseball game that evening. The software was set up with intent; it runs as designed and you accomplish your task.

When you begin to create a life that revolves around "processes," you will take a giant leap forward in short amounts of time.

Put It Into Practice

Write personal software that leads to success. Success is whatever it is you want to accomplish (such as building wealth). Run the software, run the software, run the software. You must run the software regardless of how you feel at that particular moment. Once you complete your task, you will feel different (usually quite accomplished and satisfied) as you know you did what you needed to do to move closer to your desired goals and objectives. Happiness and fulfillment will come as a result of your progress.

When you don't run your software, you won't make progress. When you don't make progress because of how you felt at a particular moment, you end up not feeling good about yourself because you know deep in your heart that you didn't do what you needed to do to reach a goal that you wanted to accomplish. You let yourself down.

Continuous adherence to proven principles of wealth success will lead to consistent breakthrough wealth over your lifetime.

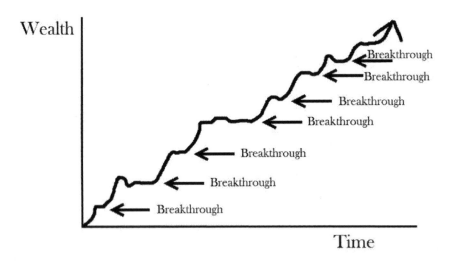

The Principles Of Wealth Success

If processes are the software steps that you run to perform a task, principles are the guiding force behind the objectives of the processes. Principles serve as the foundation for the systems. They are the reasons to run your chosen software. Principles guide our behaviors based on a mental chain of reasoning or thoughts. Base your principles on your beliefs of what it is you want to be in life.

Principles are the "why" and the "what" you want to achieve, whereas the processes are the "how." There has to be a reason "why" you want to live life in a certain fashion. Wealth builders want to accumulate wealth. That's what they want to do. It's important to them. The pursuit of wealth makes them happy (at least it should make them happy – if not, they are doing it for the wrong reasons.)

Principles act as your north star or your personal compass. They guide you in your personal pursuits. Principles should be at the core of your personal being. It's who you are. It's what your beliefs are. You should never compromise your principles based on the whims of the day or based on what others are doing or saying.

Of course, people all over the world live by different principles. Each of us may want different experiences out of our lives and that makes the entire world a better place (for the most part).

Some people want to be great musicians. Others want to provide the best medical care to those in need. Some want to be clergy members while others want to be school teachers and firemen. When you decide what is truly important to you, you can live by principles of success that become the guiding light in your pursuit of excellence.

The Principles of Wealth Success

There are 7 principles of wealth success. Wealth principles are timeless. They are like natural laws of the universe. Wealth principles work in any time generation and they don't depend on fads or current thinking. These principles were true 1,000 years ago just like they will be true 1,000 years from now.

These wealth principles are non-discriminatory. They work no matter who you are or where you were born. They work regardless of your gender or your sexual preferences. They don't take notice of your religious beliefs or your political dogmas.

It doesn't matter if you are trying to build wealth or preserve wealth. It doesn't matter if you have an exceptionally large income or a small income. These principles apply to all. Even if you are a high-earning celebrity or athlete, if you break these principles, your wealth will disappear on you in due time.

Break these principles at your own risk.

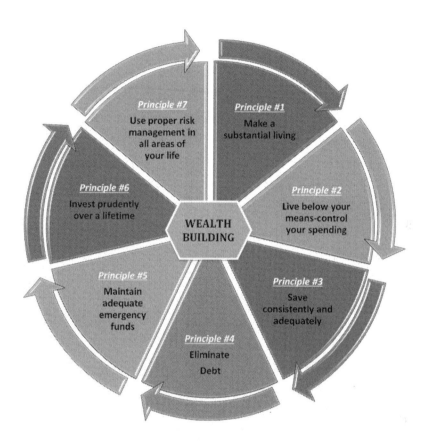

There are **Seven Principles of Wealth** that lead to success. They are:

1. **Make A Substantial Living (Generating Income).**
   Making a substantial living can mean different things to different people. Defining what someone else thinks is a substantial living isn't as important as how you define what a substantial living means to **YOU**. Are you generating enough income to reach your objectives in a timely manner that is important to you? That's what

counts. If you are on track to accumulate ample wealth over 40 years, making the income that you make, and 40 years is a period of time that you are satisfied with, then that is good enough. For you, 40 years to wealth may be appropriate. For someone else, that number may be 10 years.

2. **Live Below Your Means (Controlling Spending).**
    You will never accumulate and keep your wealth if you can't live below your means. Living below your means requires control over your spending. Failure to do so will not leave anything left over to save, invest, start new companies, and grow your wealth in ways that lead to passive income opportunities later in life. Worse yet, if you live above your means, that may require taking on debt to fund that overspending.

3. **Save Consistently And Adequately (Saving Capital).**
    Savings is required to accumulate wealth. It's not just what you make. It's what you keep after you make it. Making money is hard to accomplish. Keeping your money is **REALLY** hard to accomplish. Wealth accumulators are efficient and consistent savers.

4. **Eliminating Debt.**
    Debt leads to massive destruction of wealth more than other items because of the negative power of leverage. Leverage can be a useful tool in the accumulation of wealth. But the knife cuts both ways. It's very difficult to go bankrupt if you don't owe anybody anything. Real estate empires that have taken decades to amass can be

wiped out in short order from debt. Using debt for non-productive consumer spending is the worst kind of debt because it impacts many other areas of wealth building.

5. **Maintaining Adequate Emergency Funds.**

   You won't ever know how important adequate emergency funds are until you need them the most. Noah didn't start building the ark when the flooding was up to his knees. Emergency funds can often feel like unproductive capital because liquid assets aren't generating attractive rates of return. However, the purpose of emergency funds isn't to generate an attractive rate of return. The purpose is to provide the necessary liquidity in the event of an emergency. Once you understand and accept the reason and priority of an emergency fund, you can come to grips with the low rate of return on that capital.

6. **Invest Prudently Over a Lifetime (Managing Investments.)**

   You can be executing well in all the other areas of wealth building, but if you keep taking bad risks and losing your capital, you are forced to start all over again. This problem escalates for many reasons. First, you lose precious time. Time is our friend in wealth building because of the laws of compounding interest. Wealth grows exponentially over time. The sooner you start, the more you can accumulate and keep. Steady and prudent progress leads to larger wealth accumulation over your lifetime. Second, when you lose capital, you lose energy and get discouraged. If you keep losing your hard-earned money, you are more apt to quit and give up. At a certain point, it's just too hard to keep going and start all over again. If you invest prudently, you won't run the risk of financial explosion putting you all the way back to the start (or worse off – starting over with a pile of debt due to an investment gone south.)

7. **Use Proper Risk Management In All Areas Of Your Life.**

People often confuse this area and think that risk management is a concept to apply only to your investments. Your greatest asset is **YOU**. You must protect that investment at all costs. That means protecting different facets of yourself, including your health, skills, and reputation to name a few.

Let me provide you with two examples to demonstrate the importance of using proper and prudent risk management in all areas of your life to build and protect your wealth building. Imagine a successful CEO who finally reached the top of the company pyramid after years of hard work. At the company holiday party, he allows himself to "celebrate" a bit too much and drives home under the influence, resulting in a car crash and an arrest. He loses his job as a result of his poor behavior. Everything that he worked hard for and accomplished disappeared in short order due to very poor personal risk management.

My intention for the next example is not to provoke a political debate. But the example of a sitting President of the United States having a romantic relationship with a White House intern is an example of very poor personal risk management. If you have a situation where the upside has very little benefit, but the downside has extreme and significant ramifications, you are in jeopardy of using poor risk management in that area of your life.

Proper risk management is the opposite. Proper risk management is where the upside is huge, but the downside is very limited. Starting a new company that requires little investment capital is an example of good risk management. If the entity goes south, you lose little. But if it works, you win big. Focus your efforts on areas with proper risk management in place.

Process + Principles = Results

When it comes to wealth success there is no substitution for two key elements; process and principles. Principles tell us "why" and "what" you want to accomplish in life and the reasons for it. For wealth builders, principles are the foundations of who you are and how you choose to live.

As wealth builders, you differ from others because your principles differ from others. If someone loves watching TV and playing video games with friends while drinking beer and eating pizza, they have different life principles than you. They are doing what makes them happy. You are doing what makes you happy. One isn't necessarily better than the other unless one person is unhappy with their lives as a result of living by a certain set of principles that are in conflict with their inner desires and goals. And that, of course, would imply that their principles are flawed.

The processes that you run (personal software) should be executed based on **YOUR** personal principles, values, and beliefs. If you want to be healthy, you don't smoke cigarettes. Your personal software is about doing specific tasks, like going to the gym, that when executed prevents you from doing other specific tasks, such as hanging out at a bar, smoking cigarettes, and drinking excessive amounts of alcohol.

The Magic Of "Bum Glue"

Results and personal transformation occurs when you execute software using volume and repetition on principles that point you towards your goals. It is similar to learning to play the piano. I once asked a very good pianist what his secret to success was. Was it a gift? Was it all genetic? Was he a freak of nature? He gave me the same answer as an author I knew when I asked him similar questions about being a great author.

The secret to success for the pianist and the author was, "Bum-Glue." What is Bum-Glue? It's when you glue your bum to a chair and do the work and practice through volume and repetition. You practice, you put in your time, and you rinse and repeat. You develop principles and then you run software (processes) to execute on your principles.

Wealth comes when you practice and implement the processes that relate to principles of success using volume and repetition. If you want to save money (a principle,) then you run a process to execute on that principle (your software). What are your steps in accumulating savings in a particular account?

The more you run your processes (software) through volume and repetition, the more you will get results and transformations. Now you have "the secret sauce."

The Paradox Of Wealth

There was a once a man who thought he was doing everything right in life. He had a college degree from a good university with the student loan debt to prove it. His employer was a respected Fortune 500 corporation known for their size and history. Soon the man worked his way up the company ladder with growing responsibilities. He thought he would lead the division one day or even imagined he might be recruited by a competitor.

He made a good living and had a good paycheck. The years ticked by, but something was amiss. He couldn't quite put his finger on it. He was supposed to be living "the good life." From the outside, others would probably describe his life as the good life. But why was he discontent and unsatisfied?

His wife was happy to be in a new modernized home that they recently purchased. The new home was an upgrade from their previous home. It was a beautiful home in a wonderful neighborhood. It had multiple bedrooms. It had a finished basement and plenty of closet space. The kitchen was spacious. You could see the fairways of the community golf course while standing at the kitchen sink. The three car garage had additional space which allowed for extra storage along with plenty of room for their two new automobiles.

He was proud of the house, the cars, the boat, the clothes, the golf membership, and the expensive watch. He loved hearing compliments from others surrounding him. He reveled in the envy of others.

But he also wondered if this is how life was supposed to be. There had to be more. He wanted more. Whatever he had, it was not enough.

How could life be so mundane and stressful when he supposedly did everything right? He graduated from college. He married. He obtained a good job at a well-respected corporation. He acquired a nice house with a basement and backyard, and he drove a nice car.

He grew to feel stressed, anxious, uncertain, and confused. Isn't this supposed to be the dream? Isn't this why he worked so hard? Why was life unfulfilling?

There were many signs that all was not well. The first was a large mortgage that only had a few more decades to go before paying off. The car loans always seemed to be present. Credit card bills were a monthly routine to address as were the social gatherings that revolved around spending money.

For all the hard work and material goods that were in his possession, real wealth was escaping him. The levels of debt never diminished, they only seemed to grow over time. From the front door, he looked like a booming success but behind the front door was an unhappy man.

He as succeeding at keeping up with "The Jones's" but seemed to be failing at real wealth accumulation.

When one is stuck in that pattern, it is similar to being on a hamster wheel that is very hard to get off.

As it turns out, the paradox of wealth is that many people want financial wealth to impress others, and yet you can often obtain wealth the quickest when you stop trying to impress others.

The Weight Of The World

There was a businessman who owned three estate homes, 12 cars, a plane, and a yacht. Yet with all he had acquired, he kept working at his business that seemed to wear him out.

I asked him what it was like to balance all of those responsibilities.

He shrugged his shoulders and said, "I have a staff of 12 people on my personal payroll to keep everything going." He needed every sort of help imaginable from landscapers, pool boys, drivers, chefs, maids, a full-time captain and mate for the yacht, a pilot, and a personal assistant. And even if that sounds appealing, he said it in a way that made it sound dreadful.

"Somebody is always messing up, screwing around, or trying to take advantage of me, " he said. "There are times where I just want to sell it all and buy a small condo on the beach."

I asked him, "Why don't you sell it all, rid yourself of all of the headaches, and begin to enjoy the fruits of your labor?" He didn't answer but instead gave me a stern and annoyed look as if to say, "What, and give all of this up?"

For a person who worked hard to have it all, the complicated lifestyle made it seem as if he had nothing but the responsibilities and pressure to keep it all going.

Possessions have an interesting way of weighing you down. Each possession purchased starts with the intention of making yourself happier or making your life easier. Imagine if you had to carry everything you own on your shoulders. Sooner rather than later, it would feel as if the weight of the world was upon you. How much extra weight are you carrying around that is completely unnecessary in the greater scope of your happiness?

Successful individuals have to make brave decisions every day. They often work just as hard not to own certain possessions as they do to own certain material possessions. The point is not to avoid owning all material possessions. The point is to own very specific items that will provide the most meaning and enjoyment to you. Some of those items may be expensive. That is ok so long as you can easily afford them and the cost of ownership does not outweigh the tangible benefits and satisfaction received from ownership.

It's like being at an all-you-can-eat buffet for every meal. If you want to be healthy, all-you-can-eat doesn't mean eat-all-you can. Likewise in wealth building, you have to be willing to say no to many possessions, even if you have the means to acquire them, in order to make the possessions that you do own have an important and enjoyable impact on your life.

When you own something, get to know it – intimately. Cherish it. Treasure it. Enjoy it to the fullest. Make sure it makes a positive impact on your life. It could be as simple as a custom-built guitar or a cabin in the woods. Make that item yours and forget the rest.

Why Knowledge Alone Means Little

I'm friends with a successful entrepreneur, someone I knew well before his business took off. Within a few years of starting his business, his success levels changed dramatically. His wealth expanded faster than a waistband after Thanksgiving dinner. It was like a personal explosion of productivity was happening, and I was able to see it with my own two eyes.

The entrepreneur had a college degree and a master's degree. It wasn't one of those stories that you hear about where a person drops out of school and goes on to become a billionaire. It was a story of a person who deeply valued education and learning. He loved knowledge, and he loved reading books and articles.

I also love knowledge and learning, so I admired that aspect of him, but I also wanted more of the results that he was obtaining in life. So I swallowed my pride and asked him something that was bound to reveal a few of my personal shortcomings. I asked, "What happened that made the difference?" He said, "It's not just about the knowledge, it's about the doing."

What That Means To Me – And You

It took me a bit to comprehend what he was saying. I knew he wasn't saying that the knowledge wasn't important because it was. It's just that knowledge alone means nothing. Unless you take action and implement the knowledge into your everyday life, nothing happens. There will be no results. There will be no personal breakthroughs or transformations.

There are a lot of people out there who are stuck in this endless pursuit of more knowledge, more books, more articles, and more learning courses. They seem to hope and believe that they will start doing something productive with all of that knowledge, "once they have just a little bit more information to get started safely."

In similar fashion, there are many times where you have all of the necessary knowledge to make a good financial decision, but you will still choose poorly.

The principles of wealth success are not complicated items to understand. In reality, they are quite simple. In fact, understanding the principles is the simple part. Executing the principles daily for years on end is the hard part. Many people experience a lot of financial failure, and all too often the financial failure is self-inflicted.

The interesting perspective of my entrepreneur friend is that he is the same person he was before everything clicked and started coming together. His workday is the same as before. He likes the same activities as he liked before. He wears the same type of clothes that he wore before.

He achieved freedom and independence because he is able to do what he wants, when he wants to do it. He loves his work. He has no intention of stopping.

In some ways, I kept wondering when I was going to see him try and step out of his own skin and take on the role of "business-titan-superhero-rockstar."   Maybe he'll start tomorrow. Apparently he didn't get the memo that you need to have a hundred thousand Facebook and LinkedIn followers to be an official success story.

Choosing A Goal

Before you begin building your abundance of wealth, take a time-out and decide on a preliminary threshold well ahead of time. You don't have to set the amount of wealth you're shooting for in permanent stone. Nor will anybody fault you if you change your mind at some point down the road as your desires develop and change. But take a moment to decide what would make you feel happy, successful, and content?

Will it be when you have a net worth of $1 million? Will it be when you have a nice, paid-off home and $1 million in investments on top of that? Will it be when your net worth is $2.5 million, or $5 million or $10 million?

What does your wealth success look like in your dreams and visions? Is it a mansion and a sports car? Is it a personal staff of 12 people who need constant babysitting and paychecks? Is it a beachside condo with an amazing view of the never-ending ocean with no stress over finances ever again? Or is it the ability to go on multiple ski vacations during work breaks because you never want to stop doing what you love at work?

The starting point in any wealth plan is to select an initial wealth target number followed by a specific date to achieve that wealth target. What level of wealth meets your personal internal measure of success and accomplishment? What is that tipping point where the pursuit of one more dollar brings little additional joy to your life?

The truth of the matter is that the current goal number doesn't matter in the grand scheme of the universe. What matters about the number is that it provides a very specific, non-ambiguous, quantifiable goal you can use to compare all other factors against in your unique life.

If you are to be a wealth builder, you must commit to a path of success that every wealth builder must follow. Big goals are wonderful. Stretch goals are commendable. But they must be specific, and they must be quantifiable, and then you must do the action items and follow the processes necessary to achieve them.

Why Specificity Matters

When I work with clients new to the wealth-building process, and I ask them, "What do you want to achieve?" they usually offer one of two responses:

1. I want to be rich
2. I want a million dollars

A million dollar goal is at least specific in nature. Unfortunately though, when I follow up and ask, "Why $1 million specifically? Why not $1.5 million or $2.29 million?" they struggle on the financial details of why that number is right for them. I usually hear a response such as, "It sounded like a good answer and an adequate number."

If you don't define the wealth goals ahead of time and why those goals are important to you, you'll chase endless opportunities, enamored with all of the cash and prizes that you think those opportunities can deliver to you, and you will never be satisfied. You'll end up in the endless pursuit of "more," just for the sake of endless but unfulfilling consumption.

A wealthy life is a life of financial independence. It is a life of freedom where you control your time. It is a life where you reduce your anxieties and worries. You may discover that you need less wealth than you think if you can control your appetite for endless material consumption.

This process towards a life of independence occurs when you have knowledge. But as we discussed previously, knowledge alone won't get you there. It's in the doing. It's when you apply the knowledge in real time in the real world.

If wealth building success is only contingent upon having knowledge alone, college professors would be wealthier than most of us. But that's not the case when you think about it. That's the difference between knowing and doing. A college professor can have all kinds of knowledge from an intellectual standpoint. But what matters is how mechanisms work in the real world, in real time, with real obstacles and constraints, and still being able to execute.

It is important to balance the two objectives along the way. You must balance the learning side of the equation alongside the doing side of the equation. It's the doing and taking action that builds the actual wealth.

Remember that you are seeking to achieve breakthroughs along your journey that lead to higher levels of wealth and accomplishment.

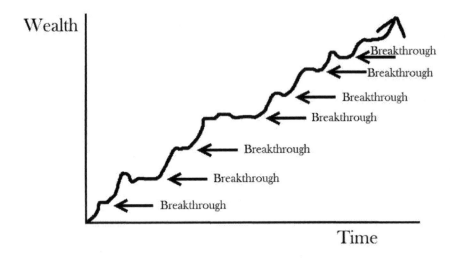

Self Reliance And Responsibility

Wealth builders are very self-reliant, and take personal responsibility for their results. In fact, these two traits are common denominators amongst successful wealth builders.

Self-reliance does not mean that wealth builders can't or don't have political viewpoints. Nor does it mean that you can't believe in God, or think that luck isn't something that happens in life.

Plenty of wealthy people have political viewpoints. Plenty of wealthy people believe in God. Plenty of wealthy people believe in luck.

But while wealthy people can believe in all those things, they also believe in themselves. They take a lot of personal responsibility for their outcomes in life.

Don't Play The Blame Game

If you are of the mindset that the reason you aren't where you think you should be in life is because of the government, your boss, your company, your friends, or your mommy, then it's doubtful you will find the self-tenacity to persevere in a lengthy process of achievement.

The biggest thing holding each of us back is often ourselves. Many life experiences could lead us astray in our journey and decision making. You may have grown up without a lot of money. You may not have had good role models. You may not have had good mentors. You may not have had the best public education growing up. You may not have had perfect parents. Your current job may stink. You may not have been given all of the knowledge along the way that it takes to figure out all of this wealth building stuff. Add to that the fact that you may have a bunch of people around you that don't want to see you succeed.

Fair enough. Those could all be true and are very reasonable issues that would describe your obstacles. But it will take individual efforts to overcome those obstacles and succeed. Nobody else is going to do it for you. Nobody is going to figure out your exact circumstances and spoon feed what you need to do in a way that you could sit back, drink a beer, relax, and ring a cash register every night.

There are countless examples of individuals who encountered great obstacles in their life yet overcame them and still went on to accomplish their wealth goals and objectives. Some of these individuals grew up poor, in broken families, with little to no formal or quality education. Others had few financial resources at their disposal along the way. But they overcame their obstacles and pursued the goals that were important to them. You must find the courage to put out that same type of effort if you want to succeed.

In health and wellness, success comes as a function of the food you eat. You are 100% responsible for what goes in your mouth. Nobody forces food down your throat. In similar fashion, you have to acknowledge that same mindset with wealth building since you have 100% control over the money that you spend and save. You have to make those decisions for yourself. You have to make those tradeoffs in life. That's part of the process.

Don't Wait For The Perfect Time

The best mindset is one where you just openly acknowledge that you have a multitude of issues that aren't ideal in your life right now. But you have to realize they aren't going to get any better unless you do something for yourself to change the circumstances.

Maybe you will have to get new friends. Maybe you will need to learn new skills. Maybe you will need to develop entirely new habits. Maybe you will need to exercise. Maybe you will need to read some books or get a second job to pay for the courses that you need to take to acquire the necessary knowledge to get you unstuck from wherever you are in your process right now.

These potential changes can certainly appear to be overwhelming and scary. They are scary. You may get nervous and afraid. You are certainly not alone in your feelings. Change is scary. Change takes time. Change takes effort. The results don't normally start appearing overnight. That is ok. Plenty of others have made the journey and are happy that they overcame their fears and insecurities.

It is not practical or efficient to try and change every single item in your life all at once. What is important is that you select one or two items that are most important to your future success and get started on those items immediately. Start today.

It's ok. It's alright. Take a deep breath. Change is good. It's uncertain. Embrace the change. Get excited about the change. Change is an integral part of the process of achievement. To make progress means constant change and evolution. If you remain in a constant state of being, there is no progress. You must be willing to help yourself because if you are waiting around in the wrong places for something good to just hit you over the head, you are not likely to progress.

"A lot of people are waiting for their ship to come in. Too bad they are waiting at the bus stop."

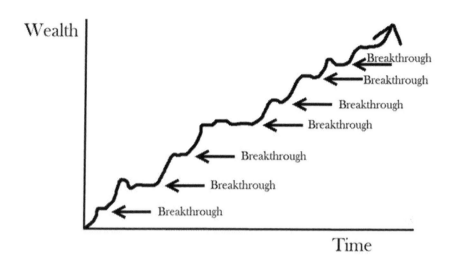

Specificity Makes Decision Making Easy

When people ask me how much money they need to retire, I explain to them, "I have no idea until I know how long you will live and what your desired standard of living is." This response usually results in a funny and frustrated face as you can imagine.

But seriously, how is one to know whether an individual will retire at 65 and die at 66 or die at 99? I ask them what they think about longevity. Some don't know because they never gave much thought to their longevity. Few people tend to plan their life in this fashion and give serious thought about the hour of their death.

I alleviate some of their confusion and uncertainty and have them complete a longevity estimator exercise. There are numerous longevity estimate tools but here's one good, free resource that I like. Go to the website – www.livingto100.com and complete the questionnaire. At the end of the assignment, you will come away with a specific number. My estimated age of death at the time I was writing this book was 97 years of age. At this stage of the game, I can say with confidence that I'm fighting for an additional 3 years to make it an even 100. I want to live to be 100 years old, intentionally and with purpose. I want to be a centenarian. I want to live a long, healthy, and active life. I live my life in a way that increases the probabilities of adding as many quality years as possible to my timeline. I hope you do too and I want to help guide you to such a wonderful accomplishment. You too should be intentional about your overall life objectives. Your life should be planned with a purpose and a game plan.

Goals Can Guide You

I have learned the importance of having very specific goals because they can help make decision making easier. Let me go back to my previous example. I want to intentionally live to 100 years of age (or older), so many habits and behaviors must be in place if I want to increase the probabilities of that happening in reality. I'm not talking about living the last 20 years drooling on myself in a wheelchair watching Wheel-of-Fortune re-runs either. I'm talking about a very long, active, and vibrant life that takes me through my 90's and possibly beyond. I want to finish strong.

I believe that we are the culmination of millions of decisions that all add up to whom we are and who we will become.

Consider the following scenarios and how to make easy decisions once you have a specific objective:

- Should I get drunk on weekends or not get drunk on weekends? Easy decision. If I want to live to 100, then I shouldn't get drunk on weekends.
- Should I eat vegetables with dinner every night or not eat vegetables with dinner every night? Easy decision. If I want to live to 100, then I should eat my vegetables.

Imagine that you had the specific goal such as living to 100 and staying as active and healthy as possible. What would you choose from the following?

- Would you get plenty of sleep each night?
- Would you exercise?
- Would you stress out on minor details?
- Would you feel compelled to make buckets of wealth overnight in some get-rich-quick-scheme?
- Would you do drugs?
- Would you pace yourself on your work career?
- Would you floss your teeth?
- Would you keep your cholesterol down?
- Would you let yourself get overweight or obese?
- Would you eat so much sugar that you developed diabetes?
- Would you drive your car 100 miles an hour?
- Would you signal to an aggressive driver that is trying to drive 100 miles an hour to pull over so you could fight him?

When you have a specific goal and are very serious and committed to that goal, many decisions become much easier to make. The same holds true for wealth building. If you have a specific wealth goal and are very serious and committed to that goal, many financial decisions become much easier to make.

Why You Should "Quit"

Having specific wealth goals stops the insanity of foolishly spending money, accumulating debt, trying to pretend to be a hot-shot, and making impulse purchases that act against your long-term self-interest.

If you decide to live a life to make it to 100 (feel free to join me), I have additional good news for you in case you aren't living up to your wealth goals just yet. I want you to quit your old mediocre life and look forward to starting over. It's not too late. In fact, since you are now going to align your decisions and actions to live to 100 (or pick your number), you probably have far more years to work with than you previously imagined.

But you must quit your old life to begin your new life as a wealth builder with a healthy foundation. Some people think that quitters never win. But that may not be true in your case because the only way that you are going to win is if you do quit being your old self.

You need to quit your old life with those old unproductive habits and behaviors and start a new life with new habits and behaviors. Those habits and behaviors must work like the software that was discussed earlier. That software leads to the execution of processes that leads to wealth and health. Those processes execute the principles of wealth success that were covered earlier (see the chapter on the Principles of Success).

Make an exception for yourself. You are allowed to quit at something without regret. You need to quit being your old self and get out of your own way. Congratulations quitter, you are one step closer to your goal of becoming a wealth builder.

When you quit all of your old unproductive habits and behaviors related to your wealth, something amazing happens. Your wealth starts moving in the direction of your newly formed specific goal. You begin to get the results that are in line with your objective. FORWARD PROGRESS AND BREAKTHROUGHS!!!

The Irony Of Wealth

Six months after implementing wealth habits and behaviors you will be picking up all kinds of momentum. Your life will get easier and clearer. The progress may even exceed your expectations. If you do the work, you will see the results. Your wealth will grow and you will have learned to escape the irony of wealth. The irony of wealth is that so many people want the wealth to impress others, but you obtain the wealth only when you stop trying to impress others.

You will like yourself more, and you will like the new processes that you put in place. You will be happier. When you are making progress towards something that is important to you, your happiness increases. Progress leads to happiness. That is how it works.

Answer this riddle for me as I have seen it in person when working with clients:

"Who is happier, a person who has accumulated their first $100,000 and is well on their way to $200,000 or a person who had $10 million to their name and is about to drop below $5 million in net worth?"

The person who doubled their wealth is excited and motivated towards a bright future. The person who lost $5 million is usually in a state of panic and experiencing paranoia. Human brains are influenced by what is called a recency bias. What we most recently experienced is extrapolated and projected into the future. Our state of wellness is often correlated to those future projections based on our most recent experiences.

Thus, we are often our happiest when we are making forward progress towards goals and objectives that are important to us. We generate the most personal fulfillment when we make strides in personal self-development and advance our state of being. When we go backwards in life, the opposite happens as it feels as though things are slipping away from us as we retreat away from important objectives.

Our happiness is tied to forward progress. Forward progress towards goals that are important to us individually leads to happiness. It is worth repeating and reminding ourselves. Forward progress and adjustments to goals will lead to breakthrough wealth.

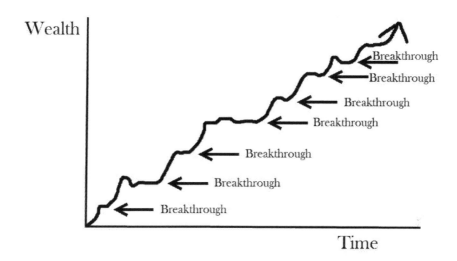

Possessions Are Not King

When you start focusing on your precious and diminishing time, your health, and your dreams, you come to an interesting realization; it's not about the "stuff."

"Stuff" and material possessions are nice. By no means should you avoid them entirely. Nice material items can be important to our satisfaction and ambition.

On one hand you may think I'm encouraging you to be weary of "stuff" and on another hand, I'm telling you that material possessions are nice. These statements may sound a bit contradictory, but let me explain further. As you focus on your limited time on earth, the people that are important to you, your passions in life, and what it is that you want to accomplish with your life, the "stuff" starts to take on a smaller role in the scheme of the bigger picture. The best items to own are those that lead to positive experiences and memories.

Focus On What Is Meaningful

It is better to focus on a few items that will greatly move the needle in your life by providing the opportunity for wonderful experiences. Pick a few items that will make the most difference in joy (rather than headaches) in your life. Those material items may be expensive, but that is ok if you can afford them. It may be a ski-chalet, a beachside condo, a fishing boat, an art studio, an antique car, or a comfy and cozy home with a garden that overlooks green pastures.

You must weigh the tradeoffs when you acquire material goods that require a lot of upkeep and responsibility. The item must provide enough joy and positive experiences that it outweighs the headaches associated with ownership. Many people get trapped in this loop. What they want is happiness. What they end up with is the opposite. They end up acquiring material items that just add more responsibility, costs, and headaches to their lives. That's another paradox of buying certain material possessions.

If you are tirelessly and endlessly working to support possessions that you can't even fully enjoy, that is a good sign that you are doing things backward.

Wealth will bring you plenty of blessings. It can deliver you the ability to control your time. It can allow you to help others that you deem important which may be family, charities, or other organizations. It can provide the very best of foods that improve your longevity. It can pay for cutting-edge healthcare with leading professionals should you need those services. Wealth can allow you to participate in all kinds of experiences that you may just not be able to do without the financial resources. With the cash come the prizes.

Don't Believe Everything You See

There are plenty of homeowners with too many bedrooms who aren't wealthy. There are plenty of people driving luxury cars who aren't wealthy. There are plenty of people with fine clothes and jewelry who aren't wealthy. Looks can be deceiving.

What you see isn't always what you get. Don't get distracted by the possessions of others. You may not ever know if they own the possessions or if the possessions own them. You would be surprised if you knew the truth and the actual statistics. The fact is, statistically, the vast majority of people are not wealthy. Very few individuals are. But as you look around, the vast majority of individuals are trying to display the signs of success. Don't be fooled. But also don't let the statistics discourage you either. You are capable of building wealth, the right way.

There will be those who build wealth faster than others. You probably won't win first place in that category. Don't be disappointed. You only have to achieve true wealth once and then have the brains not to screw it up, unfortunately this is easier said than done, and many people screw it up. There is a long list of athletes, celebrities, and business people who have blown through vast amounts of income. They were not able or willing to live by the principles of success.

Charting Your Progress

If you put in the right kind of work and effort, you will see the desired outcome. Your progress will give you adequate and appropriate feedback if you are doing the right steps along the way. You may have to make some continued habit and behavior modifications along the way. You'll welcome those changes if you still believe in your goals.

The work shouldn't be torture. Hating your life will only add to stress and anxiety. Stress and anxiety will lead to high blood pressure and other health ailments, which will show up in your periodic physical exams and provide you the feedback that you are off of the path of living to 100. Adjust accordingly.

If you are doing action items that matter, work will sometimes be hard. It will take discipline. You won't always feel like doing it. But overall you should be enjoying the process along the way because you are living a life that revolves around goals that are important to you. Your life will continue to unfold and develop. Opportunities will present themselves that you never saw coming or could have ever imagined. You'll start to become quite content with the pace of your progress. That's a sign of success.

Wealth Isn't Random   Paul Kindzia

Wealth Isn't Random

You will come across many individuals who believe that successful people are just lucky in life. They believe that wealth was handed out randomly, as if people were just blindly selected from a giant list.

Many people graduate from college, find jobs in corporate America, and then eventually expect to be hand-picked to become wealthy. These people end up extremely disappointed and confused. In their eyes, they believe that they did everything necessary and correct to have a mysterious wealth selection committee pick them so they can strike it big. When it doesn't happen, they can become angry, stressed, bitter, or jealous.

Wealthy people don't wait around to be selected randomly by somebody else. They don't put their faith in the luck of the draw. They do put themselves in favorable positions that increase the odds of success, but they work hard at evolving, adapting, and learning as they proceed towards their goals.

No Invitation Needed

The good news about joining the ranks of the wealthy is that you never have to wait for an invitation to join the club. It is open to all who complete the process of achievement, live by wealth principles, and do the work necessary. It is non-discriminating. The wealth club has no age-limits. It has no

77

race quotas. The wealth club does not care what sex you are, what religion you practice, what language you speak, or what political party you tend to favor.

The wealth club only cares if you can increase your earnings, control your spending, save and accumulate capital, eliminate, debt, maintain emergency funds, invest wisely and live your life using prudent risk management techniques. The wealth club will allow you to stay a member so long as you can live by the principles of wealth throughout your entire journey.

The principles of wealth success are universal and could be applied in any period of time, in any geography around the world. Wealth knows no boundaries. Anybody can join the club. You should join if building wealth and living your life a certain way makes you happy. Membership does come with advantages but those advantages are earned at the individual level.

CEO Of You

There are many paths to wealth. People can get there fast or slow. You could work for an employer or you could start a company on your own. It does not matter to anybody else. It should only matter to you in that you pick the method and the path that best fits your overall priorities and life objectives.

You must set a pace on your own. You must be your own cheerleader. You must hold your own performance reviews. If you think others will care about your success as much as you do, you are incorrect. Everybody loves a good success story –

but mostly if it's their own. Be your own success story. Be your own hero.

You must not wait to be a random selection out of the millions of others who are just like you, college graduates who work in a decent job. If you do, you may find yourself disappointed after long waits and no activity. Wealthy people do not wait to be randomly selected. They are picked by themselves. You must choose whether to be selected or not, and remember that wealth does not discriminate in the way that you may believe.

Wealth only discriminates and weeds out those who have not walked the path of success. There's a difference. You will learn the difference along the way.

Prior to joining the wealthy, an ongoing test requires you to execute daily processes that support the wealth principles below:

1. Generating Income
2. Controlling Spending
3. Saving Capital
4. Eliminating Debt
5. Building and Maintaining Adequate Emergency Funds
6. Managing Investments
7. Using Prudent Risk Management In All Areas Of Your Life

If you cannot live by these principles, you will not maintain your membership in the wealth club. Eliminating or failing to execute on any one of these principles can quickly lead to expulsion and suspension of your membership.

Wealth building is not a random event. It is a chosen endeavor. You choose to be a wealth builder. It is a conscious decision to continue along a path and journey of progress that leads to breakthrough wealth.

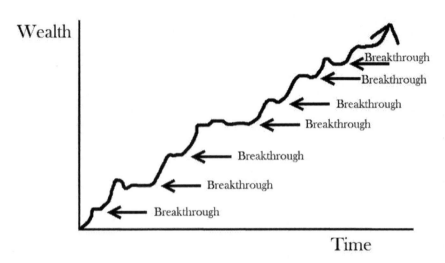

Be Professional About It

If you decide to become a wealth builder, you'll learn rather quickly that you will need to be professional about it. It does take a higher level of skill and commitment compared to the ordinary person. It requires constant training and education. Wealth building isn't amateur hour. You won't succeed if you dabble in it in your spare time.

RUNNING THE BUSINESS OF YOU

Wealth building requires you to run a business. The business will use human resources, marketing, accounting, finance, operations, and technology. The business is YOU! You must learn to operate your life like a business, serving others (your customers). You must learn to increase revenues by adding more value to your customers. You must learn to control your expenses. To elevate your income levels, you must bring more value to someone. Those that pay you for your services must know the value of what you bring to the table, which will require marketing and advertising.

You will need operational processes, which is the daily software that we discussed earlier in the book. Just like a business, you will need to perform daily tasks through volume and repetition that leads to a desired and specific result. You will need to invest in technologies no different than a business. Businesses must invest in computers, training, research, and assets, and you will have to do the same. The best businesses are constantly reinvesting in themselves to evolve and be positioned for a better tomorrow. You must take the same approach with your life. Invest in yourself.

The best businesses are run by professionals, not amateurs. Do yourself a favor and be professional about it. There isn't a successful company out there that doesn't have knowledge of their accounting and financial numbers. Successful businesses track revenues and expenses, produce projections, and perform analysis of their situation. They make investments and develop human resources.

If you aren't thinking of your life in this regard (running your life as a business serving others), you probably won't be growing your wealth very fast, if at all.

Be professional about it. If you are going to be a wealth builder, then do it. It's ok if you don't want to do it. Plenty of people have a happy life without being wealth builders. Decide if it is something that you legitimately want to do for yourself. If you think the path to wealth is going to be easy and that amateur hour techniques will lead you to a financial easy street, you may not be adequately prepared for the reality that awaits you.

Why You Need A Capital Base

Many people dream of becoming an overnight success and getting rich quick. It doesn't matter where you live, where you work, or who your parents are. Plumbers, dentists, janitors, and technology consultants all desire an easier life propelled by increased financial means.

With a global economy that includes freedom and capitalistic opportunity for billions of people, building wealth has never been as easy as it is now. It was much harder for those before us because they didn't have the knowledge and resources available to them from books and the internet that connect us all to one another. If you want to grow your wealth, you don't have the excuses and obstacles that you would have had 50 or 1,000 years ago. Nothing should be holding us back from pursuing our objectives.

What's Holding You Back?

But if building wealth is accessible by people all over the world, why aren't more people accomplishing wealth success? It's not for the lack of resources or information. Instead, it's due to a lack of core knowledge, coupled with a significant lack of the implementation of that knowledge. Wealth building is a lifestyle or a way of life in and of itself. You must choose whether you want to live your life in that fashion. You must choose to apply the tools and information that you have access to in this wired, globally connected economy.

What Is Wealth?

First, let's define the objective: What is real *wealth*?

Wealth is achieving freedom and independence. It is about obtaining full control over your time. Wealth is reaching a level in life where you get to decide what you want to do and when you want to do it. It is accomplished by accumulating the necessary financial resources to accomplish your level of freedom and independence. It is achieving a level of financial success that allows you to pursue your most important work and activities.

Wealth is a relative term because it is different for everybody. One person may determine that they need $5 million to be wealthy while another can live the life that they desire with freedom and independence with $500,000.

The Starting Point

It doesn't matter what your desired end number is, that is for you to decide what is appropriate. But regardless of your eventual desires, everyone has a starting point on initial capital. You will start with a capital base of some level, which is a starting point to build off of and progress towards your goal.

Each day, you start over again with your capital base, either growing or shrinking. A growing capital base is a core requirement for any wealth plan. If you want to accumulate $5 million, you will need to acquire $4 million before you can accomplish your goal. If you need to get to $4 million, then you must pass through $2 million first. But you can't get to $2 million if you never accumulate $1 million. You can continue this downward all the way down to zero. You will need a starting point, and for self-made individuals that starting point is usually all the same – ZERO!

Many people believe that all of the wealthy people were lottery winners or earned it the old-fashioned way (inheritance). But that is not true. The vast majority of wealthy people are self-made, and they came from very diverse backgrounds and experiences.

Your capital base is your current scorecard on your wealth destination. As it grows, you know you are heading in the right direction, making progress, and closing in on your final destination. If your capital base is not growing, that feedback is reality that you can either choose to accept or deny.

In your life, it doesn't matter where you start. What matters is where you finish. Too many people get hung up on where they are now or where they are starting from that they never do anything about their situation to progress past the starting point. You have to start somewhere. Wherever you are, start now.

It doesn't matter if you are at $100 or $100,000. If you want to get to $1 million or $5 million, you will have to progress through each number along the way. You won't go from $100 to $1,000 if you never get past $101 and then $102.

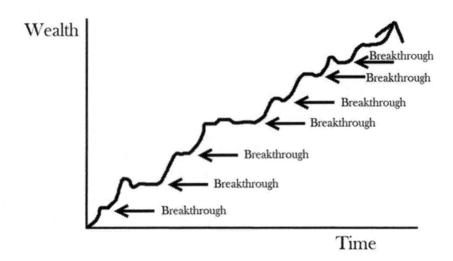

The Path Of Least Resistence

When you make up your mind to do something and commit to a goal that is meaningful to you, it makes decision-making much easier. That's how a meaningful, bottom-of-your-heart goal benefits you. It is a burning desire that makes the goal a top priority over other goals and objectives that aren't as important to you. Goals work like this in all areas of life, wealth building or otherwise.

When you commit to that goal, and you mean it and go for it, then you can make all kinds of decisions quickly and easily as you progress on your journey.

Defining Key Activities Every Day

If a young athlete says, "I want to win a gold medal in the Olympics, " and they truly mean it, that will become the GPS destination in their life navigation unit. The destination impacts the route guidance.

If the athlete is a swimmer, how do they schedule their day? What if their swimming is only done when there is remaining time after other leisurely activities? This wouldn't be the case with a competitive swimmer. Swimming would be a top priority in the daily activities which would probably include twice-daily swim practices. What does the athlete do every day? Swim. They do their laps. They do their drills. They work on technique. They do strength training. They monitor their diet, their sleep, their competition schedule. They are committed to becoming the best swimmer that they can be. They aren't joining the marching band, riding skateboards with their friends, or playing video games all day and night.

You are a product of millions of small and large decisions that you make every minute, every hour, every day, every week, month, year, and decade. Your life is just one decision after another.

- Should I watch TV or study?
- Should I work out or eat potato chips?
- Should I go home at 5:00pm or stay late to do a good job on that work project that others are relying on me to complete?

If the athlete has a deep desire and wants to win a gold medal in the Olympics one day and some friends say, "Hey, do you want to come over and get drunk with us this weekend?" then the athlete could either say, "yes" or "no," but what should be going through his or her head is, "Will this help or hurt me reach my deepest goal?"

That's why wealth builders are efficient and effective at growing their capital base over the years. They know their goal. They are committed to it. The goal never leaves their mind. Their financial goal is front and center in all that they do.

If friends say, "Hey, do you want to go out with us, spend money at the clubs, have a great time and then travel to Vegas for the weekend?" What is a wealth builder going to think? The wealth builder is immediately going to think, "Is this going to help or hurt me in getting to $100,000 or $500,000 or $2.5 million dollars?"

Goals become your compass that points to your true north.

Having a clear understanding of what you want to accomplish next in your life and what it will take to achieve that objective will lead to breakthrough wealth.

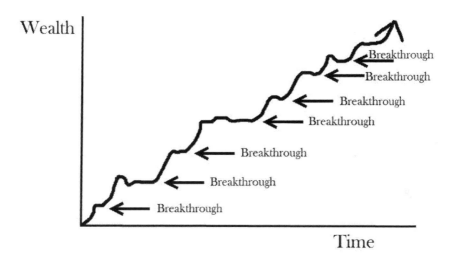

It Gets Easier With Every Dollar

One good aspect of wealth building is that it is one of the few things in life that continues to get easier as you progress to higher levels. If you ask somebody that accumulated $100,000, "Which was easier, the first $50k or the second $50k?" they usually will say that the first $50k was harder to accumulate.

The same holds true if you ask somebody who has accumulated $2 million. They will tell you that the first $1 million was harder to accumulate than the second $1 million.

Why It Becomes Easier

It becomes easier for many reasons;

1. Your capital is making money. The more capital that you have accumulated, the more money you will make on that capital.
2. You become more knowledgeable about wealth. You accumulate more tools that could be applied to your pursuits.
3. Experience allows you to recognize opportunities more efficiently.
4. You have access to business capital that could be used towards new opportunities to service others in the marketplace.

If you can imagine that you accumulated your first $100,000 and then divided it in half, the initial $50,000 was harder to accumulate because you had to figure out how to accomplish that for the very first time. But that experience provided you with a blueprint that you could repeat with confidence. If you did it once, you believe that you can do it again.

Over time, you start honing in your habits, behaviors, and skills relative to your income, spending, savings, and investments. You look for ways to do tasks and processes better, faster, and easier.

When you implement habits and behaviors into your daily life that support your long-term objectives, you end up practicing the essential elements of success in your chosen endeavor. Choices and tasks start to become automated and second nature. You don't have to think about specifics and details quite so much to make the best decisions.

Don't Be Intimidated

Take note of this reality. Sometimes when you dream big, which is encouraged, you can become intimidated by your lofty goals. The goals will seem too hard or impossible to achieve at times. If you think that they are too lofty, you can lose focus, get intimidated, and scare yourself away from continuing. A lack of confidence that results in inaction is exactly the wrong outcome that you seek.

Rather, take note that whatever you have already accumulated took more effort and energy than it will take to duplicate the same accumulation again. Saving that first $5,000 was quite hard, and you have to remember that the next $5,000 won't be as hard because you will have already learned lessons from accumulating the first $5,000.

You need to know and accept that achieving your goal will be hard, and that's exactly why people don't do it! But it gets easier along the way. The same amount of effort starts to generate bigger outcomes for yourself as you become more efficient at wealth building.

The Six Types Of Wealth Builders

In today's noisy world, you are likely to be overrun with information that is related to money, lifestyle, and the pursuits of items that are made to appear as though your life would be happy forever and ever if only you acquired them. You will be led to believe that the ownership of fine goods and services is the key to a happy life. As a result of these beliefs, it's natural for you to conclude that if you had more money right now, all would be good (or certainly better) in your life.

Two Paths To The Goal

You can pursue additional financial resources with two schools of thought in regards to personal finances. You can choose to:

1. **Make more money.** Making more money boosts our ability to spend now to acquire more goods and services. Our hope is that when we increase our spending, our level of happiness is correlated and increases as well. People often describe someone with a high income as "being rich."

2. **Build more wealth.** Wealth is something different than earning a higher income or "being rich." Wealth is robust and long lasting. Wealth is about freedom and independence. It's about doing what you want, when you want. Wealth often occurs when your accumulated capital allows you to harvest income without directly working for it. Your money is making money. When

your money is making money through passive income investments, you are not required to work constantly through active means, which takes up your precious time, in pursuit of more money that you require to sustain your chosen lifestyle.

Many Paths, One Goal

Wealth building is where the magic happens for those who figure it out. But in order to acquire and build wealth, it takes more than just earning a high income. Wealth building is a process based upon the timeless wealth principles. The results of the wealth-building process take time to emerge. These time requirements are no different than the time required for an apple tree to grow from a small seed into a large and productive fruit-bearing tree. You don't plant a seed and get fruit the following year.

What confuses many individuals about wealth building is that there are multiple approaches to the process. The principles stay consistent, but the tactics and timing can vary from one to another. Unfortunately, articles, videos, books, and how-to courses fail to explain how each method can work within the context of the various approaches to a single goal.

A wealth-building plumber doesn't approach the process the exact same way as a wealth-building technology entrepreneur. A real estate investor doesn't approach wealth building in the same way as a corporate executive does. There are tactical differences that each will apply to their situation.

Deciding to become a wealth builder is the important first step in the process. It is a choice you must make and commit to. After that, you need to decide "the type of wealth builder" that is best for yourself. Before you start laying out your plan, you should decide which approach that you want to take and best fits your life objectives and personality.

The following is a brief description of the six types of wealth builders.

The Frugal Fanatic

The Frugal Fanatic takes an approach of saving and accumulating capital through the constant sacrifice of a reduction in spending. It's all about cutting expenses and spending less money. Finding ways to increase revenue or income takes a back seat to spending time on finding ways and methods to constantly cut expenses.

The Frugal Fanatic will spend time cutting coupons, chasing sales, and the endless pursuit of bargains as a way to spend less and save more.

The Worker Bee

The Worker Bee is someone who works as an employee as their primary source of income generation and works within the system and environment of their employer. The Worker Bee is diligent about executing the principles of wealth but is content with taking the longer path to capital accumulation. Worker Bee's accumulate wealth over long periods of time (decades).

The means to wealth is usually through publicly traded stocks, bonds, and employer retirement plans (that also utilize stocks and bonds as the driver of long term wealth).

The Worker Bee usually has a wealth goal that relates to a retirement that will begin after a long career lasting multiple decades, approximately 40 years, and will move steadily and consistently along the path of accumulation.

The Master Craftsman

The Master Craftsman is more of an independent producer who has pursued skills and abilities that allow him or her to work outside of traditional corporate employment. Master Craftsmen spend extra time at the beginning of their career honing their desired craft into a level of expertise that allows for higher earnings once those skills are fully developed and valued by society.

Examples of a Master Craftsman would include a CPA, a dentist, a plumber, a home builder, or an orthopedic surgeon.

Master Craftsmen can often generate and earn higher incomes compared to others who work in traditional employment situations. And beyond additional earnings, they are not as liable to be subject to layoffs, or careers that are dependent on the whims of large employers who try to manage annual corporate earnings from year to year and are constantly forced to improve efficiencies and do more with less. Master Craftsmen are most often self-employed and can enjoy long careers without employment interruptions or early terminations which can be typical in a corporate based career.

Master Craftsmen take a longer term road to wealth through consistent and higher paying self-employment. They eventually look to retire once they no longer have the desire and energy to continue working in their chosen field. However, many Master Craftsmen enjoy their trade and profession and continue to work into old age out of the sheer enjoyment of their craft and profession.

The General
Generals are those who seek to expedite their wealth-building process through superior earned income that allows them to save unusually high percentages of their annual pay.

Generals are those who work hard and spend energy on getting promoted up the ranks of an organization as quickly as possible. Generals work for organizations (and hence are employees) but become the leaders of those organizations.

Generals can be employed across all kinds of institutions and organizations such as for-profit corporations, the military, hospitals, universities, not-for-profit institutions, or government entities.

Generals work hard to acquire the leadership, political, and technical skills to speed up the wealth-building process. This is done through superior income generation compared to the income of others. Generals have high earned-income levels and can quickly accumulate wealth at expedited rates so long as they keep their personal expenditures within reasonable yet enjoyable levels.

The Business Owner

Business owners are independents, much like Master Craftsmen. They desire having full control over operations, systems, processes, and resources. Business owners are focused on solving problems in the marketplace. They often are less concerned with "what the business does" relative to personal passions versus how to maximize economic opportunities and profits.

Business owners seek high amounts of personal compensation and the opportunity to build significant value when the company could be sold to another entity.

Business owners span the entire economy from manufacturing to services. They could own a business that supplies Port-O-Potty's or they could manufacture widgets used in other products. Business owners are more attracted to the opportunities to serve others (individuals or other businesses). They actively seek to hire and employ others to help service the needs of the marketplace as the world continues to change.

Business owners are less interested in investing in stocks and bonds and much more interested in investing capital in their own businesses that they control. Business owners make up a significant amount of the wealth population.

The Rebels

Rebels are the die-hard independents, the crazies, the entrepreneurs, the misfits, and the high-risk takers that refuse to follow the rules or work for others. Rebels are looking to change the world and create organizations that solve problems for society that have not yet been solved or invent products and services not yet imagined. They are true originals.

Rebels are on the cutting edge and are usually disrupters to other traditional businesses and industries.

Rebels often earn very low pay for sustained periods of time while they build something of value from scratch and normally with elevated risk/return profiles. Their endeavors can fail spectacularly, or they can be rewarded handsomely if the venture proves to be a success.

Rebels do not use a "slow and steady" approach to wealth building like Worker Bees and Master Craftsmen. Rebels often have to live like Frugal Fanatics while they chase their dreams and venture ideas.

Rebels often appear to be "overnight successes" but their successes rarely come "overnight" or without tremendous risk and sacrifice for years on end. However, it only takes one successful venture to create permanent wealth that could last more than a lifetime if properly managed.

The largest, quickest, and youngest wealth accumulators are usually successful Rebels.

What type of wealth builder are you right now? What type of wealth builder most resonates with your core personality and desires? There may be times when you are attracted to a particular type (such as a General or Rebel) because of a certain glamour or expedited route to wealth. But you must also be willing to live the life of those types, which you may find to be unattractive and not in your core being. You may want the wealth results of one type, but you will not be satisfied or happy with the daily lifestyle required to reach those results using that type. You must accept the trade-offs that you need to make in your life based on your personal desires and preferences.

Think carefully about the type of wealth-builder that you want to be. Your happiness depends on it. Remember that there are numerous ways to succeed at the wealth-building process and that your objective is to choose the method that fits your personal preferences the best.

Model A Plan, But Make It Your Own

Now that you have discovered the six types of wealth builders, you need to pick the one that is best suited to your personal needs and desires. Nothing says that you can't one day morph from a Worker Bee to a General, or from a General to a Business Owner, but you will have to start somewhere to get going on your life path.

The most efficient and effective path to wealth is to model, but not copy, others who have chosen to be a similar type of wealth builder. Attempting to copy the exact route of another is where a lot of the confusion comes from as you read up on the information that is out there related to money and finances. Not all tools, tactics, and approaches apply to all people or all of the six types of wealth builders. They need to be customized to fit the specific person and application.

Different Types, Different Tactics
When you understand the type of wealth builder you are and the path you choose to follow, you can then start to determine and implement the tools and tactics that best fit your chosen style of wealth accumulation.

The tactics and tools that you choose to employ must be applicable to your chosen wealth accumulation type. Otherwise you end up spending time and resources on activities that don't make a hill of beans' difference in the scope of your life and happiness.

Here are a few examples to provide perspective. If you were to search on the internet for a common financial topic like, "Should I do a ROTH IRA conversion?" you will get more than two million results from Google. It's a very popular tactic that people discuss and read about in articles.

But let me ask you this, "If you were a Rebel building a company, would spending time and resources on ROTH IRA conversions be the most pressing and important item in your chosen wealth style?"

Of course it would not be important at all. Donald Trump and other real estate moguls didn't get rich because they did a ROTH IRA conversion. Nor are they rich because they maxed out their 401k each year. Those weren't the catalysts of their success. Rather, their time, effort, and energies were spent in ways consistent with a Business Owner within the real estate market. They made their wealth using different tactics than a Worker Bee or Master Craftsman would use.

Use Models, But Customize

The point is that each of us needs to model our wealth plan based on what works for the chosen path you decide to take for yourself. You also need to make that wealth plan your own because as you will learn, "We are all the same, but we are all different."

Nobody is going to have the exact circumstances as you have nor have the exact same personal preferences and priorities. Nobody else is going to have your exact career, your exact home, your exact car, your exact health needs, your exact hobbies, or clothes or family situation. Those are all unique to you.

The important point is that there are many successful wealth builders who employed methods that were based on similarities to you, but not exactly the same. Your situation will be slightly different but some tactics will be worth modeling and implementing in your own game plan.

You want to model yourself to make the most efficient use of other successful examples, but make the final plan unique to your personal set of circumstances and individual priorities. That is the most effective and efficient way to experiencing a breakthrough to a higher level of wealth and transforming your life. Otherwise, you run a great risk of not being happy in life because you aren't living the life that is best suited for you.

Modeling correctly is important to grasp as it is the reason some wealth builders are not happy with their lives. You often hear that, "Money doesn't buy happiness." But more often than not, the root of the problem isn't the wealth itself. It's the way the person lived their life in pursuit of wealth. If you aren't enjoying your life along the journey, that is a good indication that you are on the wrong track.

Your wealth goals have to be congruent with your overall life purpose. Your wealth plan has to put you on a journey that is right for your unique view of the world and how that relates to your individual life. All wealth builders have something in common, they want to build and accumulate wealth.

But then each wealth builder has to go on their separate path to accomplish that goal through the life that is best suited for them. You will have to follow the principles of success. You must individualize the tools and tactics that you use and the processes you follow to enjoy the journey and enjoy the breakthroughs. Otherwise, you will end up building wealth, but you will not enjoy the process and will go through life being unhappy and discontent.

The Three Great Goals Of Wealth Planning

There are three main goals that you should seek to accomplish within your overall wealth plan. These are three very specific objectives that will clear up a lot of confusion once you understand the framework behind them. The three great goals of wealth planning are:

1. Accumulate enough capital to sustain yourself indefinitely.
2. Eliminate all debt.
3. Accumulate and maintain adequate emergency funds.

If you can accomplish the three great goals of wealth, it should result in your ultimate objective which is obtaining freedom and independence.

The First Great Goal of Wealth Planning

The first great goal of wealth is to accumulate enough capital to sustain you indefinitely. Approaching a wealth amount from this perspective provides the answer to the sought-after question, "How much do I need to be wealthy?"

As you accumulate enough capital to sustain yourself, your efforts can move towards your deepest purposes and passions rather than towards efforts to work on tasks and projects, "just for the money."

When you have accumulated capital, you can invest that appropriately in vehicles that will generate passive income. Passive income comes from investments that generate dividends, interest, capital gains, cash flows from privately owned businesses, or revenue such as rental income.

When you have income from multiple sources, and if many of those sources don't require you to work directly on them (hence they are defined as "passive income"), then you make your financial house more robust. Likewise, if you only have income from one source, and that source is a paycheck from a job that you actively need to perform each day and week, your financial house can be described as being more fragile.

In wealth building, you seek to build a robust approach, rather than a fragile approach.

The Second Great Goal of Wealth Planning

The second great goal of wealth is to eliminate debt, especially non-producing consumer and consumption based debt. Debt is a very touchy subject for many people because they may already have very strong beliefs about the topic before they begin to understand how debt fits into creating the robust financial situation that is particularly valuable in retirement or even pre-retirement for that matter.

Debt entails fixed expenses, and typically large, consistent, and long term fixed expenses. When you owe money to others, especially corporate lending institutions like banks, auto financing companies, credit card issuers, and mortgage lenders, they don't care what is happening in your life.

Lenders don't care if you don't like your boss or your job. Lenders don't care if the industry that you work in is going through a permanent transformation. Lenders don't care if the company needs to restructure or reorganize, which results in heads rolling. If you lose your job, you lose your paycheck, and when you lose your paycheck, lenders don't care. Lenders want their debt repayments PLUS INTEREST each and every month.

As people age, they often have the desire to simplify and keep things safe and secure. You are likely to want your life to be more robust and less fragile. As people age, they usually prefer predictability and routine. They don't like uncertainty because uncertainty provides opportunities to worry. Who wants to worry about money and finances as you ride into the sunset of your career and life?

My prediction is that you will prefer to spend your time focusing on your passions and purpose as soon as possible. Whether or not you achieve this goal will be up to you. Eliminating debt is another way to make your financial life more robust and less fragile.

The Third Great Goal Of Wealth Planning

The third great goal of wealth is to build and maintain adequate emergency funds. What you learn as you proceed through life is that "stuff happens." The main weapon to aid us when "stuff happens" is to have adequate emergency funds on hand at all times. This means having access to ample amounts of liquid cash.

There are countless examples of situations that can affect us over the span of our lifetimes. You can lose your job unexpectedly, get a flat tire, find your refrigerator leaking, have your air conditioners give out in the heat of summer, or experience a health situation that arises out of nowhere.

Most individuals act completely surprised when negative situations arise. You should expect issues and obstacles to arise in the normal course of life. Nobody proceeds through life without challenges. If you can prepare for unexpected events ahead of time, you can navigate them while avoiding finding yourself in crisis mode without adequate resources. Extra financial resources are quite useful when you need them the most.

Emergency funds can be a combination of cash kept at home, along with liquid cash resources at financial institutions. Do not invest emergency funds in volatile securities or illiquid investments. Examples of appropriate places for emergency funds would include checking accounts, savings accounts, or money market accounts.

Emergency funds must be liquid, and you must be able to access them quickly without penalty or risk of loss. Many households make the mistake of investing emergency funds in volatile securities like stocks only to discover that they need those funds precisely when stock markets are volatile and not cooperating. That forces them to sell stocks at losses.

When you build up and maintain adequate emergency funds, you make your financial houses more robust and less fragile.

A Robust House

When you accomplish the three great goals of wealth, you have made your financial house very robust and less fragile.

You have created multiple streams of income that is not contingent upon you working for a paycheck.

You have eliminated all significant fixed expenses resulting from debt payments that lenders would require you paying regardless of circumstances.

Finally, you have provided yourself with a financial reserve fuel tank that gives you some breathing room when unexpected events happen (and they will happen to you). You won't be forced to sell any investment or holding to generate much-needed liquidity to meet your core variable expenses.

Noah didn't start building the ark when the water was up to his waistline. You may not need an entire ark, but it's best to buy an umbrella before it begins to rain.

Wealth Habits Are Learned And Developed

There are many who believe that wealth is random or based on luck. Many may not want to acknowledge that wealth building requires a mix of skill and direct intention with specific actions, and there are reasons different individuals enjoy various wealth levels.

You need to build wealth using a proven process of achievement. The process is something that must not only be learned but developed and implemented into your daily life for the results to occur.

Success Comes From Habits

Successful wealth builders create a standard on how they want to live their lives. Establish your standards and then relentlessly follow that standard until your goals are achieved.

Wealth building is like many endeavors that can be replicated and achieved with a process.

Success in any endeavor has much to do with behaviors and habits and the implementation of key variables. Small changes in behavior often lead to substantial differences over long periods of time. It is no different from the process of wealth building. Success and progress are expedited when you spend appropriate amounts of time focusing on habits, behaviors, and fundamentals.

Wealth builders strive to establish and implement goals that are both short term and long term in nature, and which focus on events and items that they can control in their lives. They don't spend a lot of time and effort on events that they simply cannot control, such as fretting about politics or the global economy.

Time Will March On

The success of their methods stems from their ability to create a personal process, a system, whereby wealth building results from executing habits that accrue benefits over the normal and unstoppable passing of time. One way or another, time is going to pass. Let this work in your favor.

Discipline, hard work, and the ability to execute a process will separate the achievers from the non-achievers. After all, high achievers are exposed to the same tax system, have the same government, invest in the same global markets, and are subjected to the same global economies. Thus, ask yourself, "Why do some succeed while most don't if we are all living in the same environment with the same opportunities?"

Every high achiever is busy. High achievers are usually busier than others. Every high achiever has a career, family, hobbies, activities, and priorities. Wealth builders simply consider wealth accumulation a top priority and are willing to do the necessary work to follow the process. Wealth building takes dedicated time and effort. Like most things in life, the successes that are most satisfying often require time, effort, and hard work.

You would be wise to think about where you want to be five or ten years from now. What kind of life do you want to be living? What kind of wealth do you want to accumulate? Start making incremental progress towards those objectives. The path will often be hard but the time will tick off the clock regardless of what you do.

One way or another, five and then ten years will slip past you in your life. At that point, you will either be glad that you ended up at your desired destination, or you will be filled with regret when you realize that you are in the same position that you were in years ago. Regret is often the result when you change nothing in your life. If you still desire a different result later in life, you will have to face the exact situation as before. Are you willing to do the work to obtain your results or will you choose to change nothing and wind up wasting another five or ten years?

"A year from now you may wish you had started today." –
Karen Lamb

The Haters, Baiters, And Non-Believers

Unfortunately, wealth building isn't always an easy task within your family and social circles. That may sound odd, but it is true. The fact is, not everybody will want you to succeed, but it will be for various reasons that may not have occurred to you before starting your journey. You will experience many social circumstances along the way, so it's best to be prepared for those ahead of time.

Being aware of wealth-related social circumstances will allow you the opportunities to stay focused and to have the confidence that you are indeed doing the right tactics FOR YOU.

Listed below are three types of individuals with whom you will cross paths with along your journey. It will benefit you to understand these personality behaviors ahead of your encounters with them. Knowledge of their typical behaviors will allow you to navigate social situations as a wealth builder with greater ease and comfort.

Haters Are Going To Hate

"Everybody loves a good success story, unless it's not their own."
– Paul Kindzia

Haters have a tendency to want to knock another person down a few notches. This vitriol or bitterness could come in many different forms, such as a snotty comment, a glance of disdain with rolling of the eyes, or gossip among your peer group. Haters are like the trolls on the internet who would rather spend their limited time on earth bringing somebody else down or criticizing another person rather than spending that time to improve their personal situation.

Humans have a behavioral tendency to believe that each of us is at the center of our own universe. Further, it's human tendency to compare our universe against the universes of those closest to us in social or family relationships. It's in our nature to compete. Competition is nature's way of working her magic where the strong survive and pass on the best genetics.

Instinct makes us compete. We compete for food and jobs. We compete for material possessions. But at our core, we compete for sex, mates, and social status. It just so happens that humans have evolved in ways that isn't as obvious as peacock feathers and elk antlers to display superiority among competitors. Rather than long and colorful peacock feathers to display our excellence, humans implement a mix of material possessions such as clothes, cars, jewelry, or houses to display their social ranking.

At its core, money and the appearance of wealth represents success and power for men along with power and security for women. It's in our DNA. Men want to be strong, powerful, and successful. Doing so increases their odds in attracting those of the opposite sex (Men, how often have we seen TV infomercials selling us a get rich quick scheme so, "You too can own a yacht full of bikini-clad bombshells!")

Women are attracted to strong, powerful, successful men as it provides the best chances of security that is programmed into their DNA. The purpose of stating this (which may appear to be obvious by some) isn't to create a social argument. Women and men alike can be very capable and happy wealth builders. The point is to understand human behavior at its core.

When you move up the wealth ladder, you are altering the current dynamics of your social circles and peer groups. If you move up, well then what does that mean for those who now are below you on a social dynamic scale? What are they going to think of the situation? Are they going to go out of their way to say, "Congratulations for making me look less attractive to my peers, co-workers, company leaders, family members, community, and my potential mates?"

Haters won't be able to match your real output or progress. Therefore, they are limited by words or actions against you. The best thing you can do is accept it as a sign of achievement. Remember, you aren't trying to make others look bad. You are trying to improve yourself and make progress along your journey.

There will be breakthroughs that you achieve along the way that will be noticed by others during your journey. It's like getting in shape and working out. After two days of working out, others aren't going to notice anything different about you. But after a few weeks, they will begin to say, "There is something different about him/her." After a few months, it's clear to everybody, "That person has it going on!"

When you get in better physical shape, it's more than just visual. It changes your soul. You know you evolved into a different person, and thus, you carry yourself differently. You will become more confident. You will become more content. You will become more energetic. You will feel the changes and others will pick up on it as well.

The same holds true with wealth. When you start getting your financial house in order and building those financial assets (muscles) and losing that debt (fat), you and everybody around you will notice something different. These changes may be threatening to others.

I want to share one tidbit that relates to haters. This tidbit comes from Coach Nick Saban, one of the most winningest college football coaches of all time. He has coached national championship teams at different universities and was rated by Forbes Magazine in 2008 as "The Most Powerful Coach in Sports." Here's what Nick Saban would share with his teams:

"Mediocre people don't like high achievers. High achievers don't like mediocre people." – Nick Saban

You always see interesting human social dynamics at work when you start mixing high achievers with low achievers. Both will be annoyed with the other side but for the opposite reasons. You need to decide which camp you want to settle in and go from there.

When haters hate, be patient, be proud, and understand the deeper context of the situation to avoid conflict.

Baiters

Baiters create a different social dynamic than haters. A Baiter is somebody within your family, peer group, or social circle who tries to entice you to make bad financial decisions.

Have you ever been on a diet and been around people who constantly make comments like, "Just have one, " or "You can have a little," or "But it's a birthday party, so eat some cake."

Those are Baiters.

Staying true to your wealth plan is hard. But when you see your family, friends, neighbors, and co-workers spending money like it is going out of style, it may become tremendously hard to execute your wealth-building plans. Your feelings, determination, and focus can deteriorate when people whom you either like or are forced to be around due to social dynamics place pressure on you – either subtle or not-so-subtle – to throw your wealth plans out the window and "eat the proverbial chocolate cake for breakfast."

It is essential that you visualize and rehearse for these social situations, which are bound to arise and can make you feel quite awkward. What do you do when everybody at work says, "We are going out for dinner and drinks after work. Do you want to come?" and you say, "I'm not wasting my money on food and drinks. I have a savings goal this month."

What does this imply to the others?

It's important that you are sensitive to others with whom you spend time along your journey. Most people struggle with personal finance issues. People think about money more than almost any other issue in their lives. When you say, "Hey, I've got goals; I've got a plan; I'm disciplined; I'm going to be a success," and you stick to your guns, how is that making others feel about themselves?

Wealth builders are not the only people who are trying to deal with change. Wealth builders just happen to be those who are capable of implementing the changes necessary to achieve the accumulation of wealth. That leaves the remainder wanting more money and financial resources, but struggling with making the life changes necessary to achieve the result.

As scared as you are of making necessary changes in your life, others are just as scared. That often results in them becoming Baiters because if they see others changing for the better, that would mean that they have to change themselves. If that person is not ready to make those changes, it can make them feel resentful and bitter towards you for ruining their chocolate cake breakfast and poor financial behaviors.

In essence, people don't want to see their friends turn down a drink or a piece of chocolate cake because that might mean that they have to change. They will need to resolve the inner conflict within themselves to tackle change and may not be as ready as you were. Thus, these issues are about them, not you.

When dealing with Baiters, the best thing to remember is that it isn't about you as much as it is about them. You need to take their behaviors, actions, and comments for what they are: a camouflaged compliment that may appear as a dig or sabotage against you. Be proud; take note; and be sensitive; but stick to your guns.

Non-Believers

"The streets will flow with the blood of the non-believers."

Along your wealth journey, you will come across and will have to deal with plenty of non-believers.

Non-believers are similar to Haters and Baiters. The issues are very similar to the core social and psychological behaviors of human dynamics. Nobody was born a pure wealth builder. Wealth building is a process that has to be honed based on habits and behaviors. Wealth building is the implementation of rock-solid, time-tested, and proven principles of success.

You have heard the stories of people going from rags to riches. People may want to believe that the reason they aren't wealthy is because they didn't grow up with a silver spoon in their mouth. That is a common misconception, but that is not how the world works. It is natural to desire an easy path such as being born into or inheriting wealth. But that is not the common path for the vast majority of wealth builders.

Hard work along with the acquisition of skills over time is not something that many want to believe in, and that is what makes them "non-believers."

Wealth builders all have to learn and implement the same skills as other wealth builders. They may do it in different ways or for different periods of time, but the core curriculum is similar for wealth builders.

Non-Believers are like those who hear you are on a diet and will lash out and say, "Oh, give it a week and you'll be back to eating chips and ice-cream."

Non-Believers don't want to see the permanent and beneficial change in others because it would rock their internal belief system. If they were forced to acknowledge that change was possible in somebody else, it would imply that change is possible within them (if they would only put in the effort to change). Since they are not willing to make changes within themselves, it only makes sense that they are Non-Believers with others who are attempting change.

Non-Believers tend to come across as Debbie-Downers or Negative-Neds. They won't have a single word of encouragement for you. Rather, they will express their internal belief system on you in hopes that you don't change. The non-believers will exhibit this behavior so that they don't feel bad about themselves for not making the effort to change.

You have to remember that most of the people around you have similar backgrounds. They may have grown up in the same family, or the same neighborhood, attended the same schools, or work in the same company. There is typically a lot of common ground between you and your social circle. When you change, it rocks the order and stability of their known universe.

If everybody in your group is convinced that they could never become wealthy because of their employers, their upbringing, or the government, and you come in and prove otherwise, that's a hard thing for them to come to grips with because it exposes the flaws in their belief system, thus creating internal conflict within them.

That will force many to either change themselves (highly doubtful) or create a loophole for their behavior system by stating that the success of someone else was due to luck or randomness. An attitude or belief such as this is a common behavioral response when somebody else isn't ready or willing to change. It feels safer and more comfortable for them to do nothing and wait for luck or randomness to change their reality.

Unfortunately, life doesn't reward this type of inaction or stagnant behavior.

At the core of the social issues is a change in dynamics. Change is hard for everybody. Further, you need to acknowledge that your changes within yourself impact others whether it is directly or indirectly. If you are married or are a parent, and you are making financial changes, I can assure you that your new habits and behaviors will impact others, since you may want to save more money rather than spend it. Spouses and children may not like that change and will fight you on it because they aren't ready for the change or don't see the benefits of change that you do.

A Strategy That Works For All Three

Whether you are dealing with Haters, Baiters, or Non-Believers, you may find it useful to respond to others by describing your new values and not the desired outcomes. When people nudge you to make poor financial decisions, a lot of what they say falls into the, "Oh, come on, spend a little money and have some fun. You have to live for today. You could be dead tomorrow," category. Some people can be rather pushy and aggressive in unexpected ways.

It may be helpful to state your new values positively, such as, "I want to improve myself," or express yourself in regards to your feelings such as, "I am feeling excited about my progress." People have a much harder job when it comes to disputing or attacking feelings. What are they going to say, "No, you don't feel excited about making progress because I said so?" This approach accomplishes two objectives. It not only has a better chance of shutting down a pushy person, but it also reminds you of what you truly and deeply want to accomplish.

It is possible that you will lose friends as you build your wealth to new and higher levels. Keep in mind that you can make new friends who share your desired values. You cannot get a do-over in life for wealth building. The days, weeks, and years will continue to expire and become the past. Friends, acquaintances, and co-workers will come and go, but you must ensure that your wealth-building efforts do not do the same. You must adhere to your personal set of values and principles.

To summarize and remind you once again before moving on, when you run into social dynamics with Haters, Baiters, and Non-Believers, you should take the instigation of others as a deeper hidden form of compliment. What it means is that people are taking notice of your progress at a level where it is impacting their behavior and emotions.

KEEP UP THE GOOD WORK!

Don't let others distract or discourage your from you own goals and objectives in life. Breakthrough wealth is possible when you stay true to yourself and your commitment to your own path.

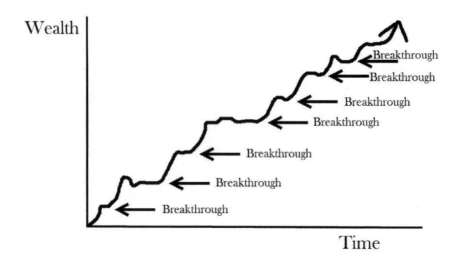

There Isn't A Preseason In Wealth Building

Once you make that jump across the line and officially commit yourself to being a wealth builder, you accept and welcome the process as a lifelong journey. As a wealth builder, you must develop and live by your individual code of conduct required for success. Wealth building isn't a part-time endeavor. It requires a high level of consistent commitment. Most of all, you have to be professional about it.

There isn't a preseason in wealth building and there are no practice games. What you do each day, each hour, each minute means something. Time is ticking off of your life clock. Every day is a playoff game. But that doesn't mean that you won't make mistakes, have setbacks, or fumble the ball. That is part of the process.

Wealth building requires a constant state of diligence. Being committed, strong, focused, and goal-oriented 99% of the time won't end well if 1% of the time you go and buy a luxury car using debt or decide to upgrade your personal residence to keep up with your brother-in-law or co-worker. If you make poor decisions that are large enough in magnitude – even only 1% of the time, you can still unravel the good that you created the other 99% of the time. Human emotions are very capable of breaking us down 1% of the time.

The required focus and constant commitment is no different than that required for nutrition and weight loss. You can't eat healthy and nutritious foods 99% of the time and then eat an entire pizza and chocolate cake and expect to lose weight. It doesn't work like that. Moderation and discipline are necessary over long periods of time to achieve success.

A few decisions can have lifelong impacts on your outcome. Wealth building is a lifestyle that requires unwavering commitment on items that will tempt all of us. The irony of wealth is that people typically want it to impress others, but they can only obtain it when they stop trying to impress others.

Further, when you work hard and make sacrifices, you may often feel entitled to some rewards, and you are. It's just that you cannot succumb to the desire for immediate gratification every time you feel tired, worn-out, or frustrated by the patience required for the endeavor. Each time you give in financially to something that appears to be a strong craving but isn't in alignment with your long-term goals, it is just like eating the chocolate cupcake when you are on a diet because you are tired, worn-out, and feel that you deserve a treat.

Write down your goals, including the smaller items that you desire. Write down what it is you need to achieve before making those expenditures. For example, maybe you reward yourself with a small splurge after reaching a milestone. You must ensure that you are acting in line with your objectives and not giving in to impulsive and emotional decisions that can quickly derail your best laid out financial plans.

Smaller rewards that are planned and deserved (and earned) are fine along the way. But once you start the process of wealth building and get the ball rolling, it's game-time. It's the playoffs. Play your best game and be proud of yourself for giving it your all.

Remember, becoming a wealth-builder is a conscious decision. It is a choice. It is a lifestyle. You are doing it to make yourself happy.

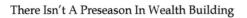
There Isn't A Preseason In Wealth Building   Paul Kindzia

You Will Need To Track Financial Data

"What gets measured gets done."

If you aren't benchmarking your progress, how will you know if you are making the proper progress at the appropriate speed?

In a prior chapter, we discussed the importance of being professional. You have to approach your life as a wealth builder like running a business. Can you imagine a successful corporation operating without measuring any results? Would they fire the accounting department? Would they lay off the finance department? Would there be a need for quality control? Would they inform human resources that there will no longer be performance reviews or assessments of efficiencies by anybody?

Run Your Wealth Building Like A Corporation

How successful do you think an organization would end up being if they didn't track or measure progress and results? Why is it that people believe that it should work any differently in their personal life?

When you get serious about wealth building, you will also have to get serious about tracking financial data related to your plan to monitor your results and transformation. Examples of financial matters to take into account include:

- Your income

- Your taxes and rates of taxation
- Your spending by categories
- Your savings
- Your debt levels
- Your net worth
- Your investment balances and rates of return
- Your monthly and annual comparisons for benchmarking
- Your checking and savings account balances
- Your automobile details and funding for future cars
- Your projections and outlooks for future years and time periods

Many techniques, tools, and resources are available for wealth builders. An example would be Quicken software that helps track your income and expenditures or using spreadsheets to benchmark comparisons. Look into the details and pros and cons of different options and what will work best for you, as it's worth mentioning that as you progress, so will your need for tracking and benchmarking.

Progress Will Lead To Results

Results and transformations occur when you quantitatively see progress occurring and then you make the correlations as to why results are happening. Once people learn to "connect the dots" and "follow the bouncing ball," on how financial items relate to one another and how certain actions result in certain outcomes, the speed of progress increases tremendously.

It's very similar to tracking your diet in terms of calories, sugar, carbohydrates, fats, protein, and sodium. When you eat adequate nutrient-dense foods, limit sugars, and exercise, it doesn't take long for you to notice. You will start thinking, "Hey, this is interesting. My weight and cholesterol levels are diminishing, and I look better in the mirror. I also have more energy and can think more clearly."

The same holds true with financial tracking. When you monitor your expenses, and see that your wealth is increasing, your investments are increasing, and your savings are increasing, you will start to notice how the results occur. Discovering the catalysts of wealth building will lead you to execute and behave in ways that generate preferred results. Patterns will emerge. Over time, you hone your habits and behaviors to maximize the output with the inputs that you have developed.

Tracking your inputs will influence your outputs. Obtaining the desired outputs will lead to breakthrough wealth.

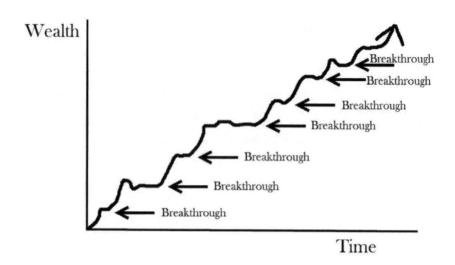

One Step At A Time

Most people struggle with their finances. Unfortunately, the human brain isn't wired correctly for natural financial success so our brains are often working against us.

Humans are very social creatures, like all primates, in addition to being emotional. Humans are wired to seek out security, food, and reproduction. A lot of hardwiring is at play when humans make decisions that most people don't understand.

We Are Wired For Immediate Gratification

Corporations understand this when they market and advertise to us. They have become extremely effective and efficient in motivating us to make purchases of goods and services that we believe will make us happy, safe, or attractive.

Wealth building is a process and a progression of skills. It's important to think of it this way so that you don't get discouraged and quit before all the good factors start working for you. It's very similar to the overall education process that you went through as a child. In childhood education, you progress from one grade to the next by building off of the skills previously acquired.

That's why I often say the following;

"Don't compare your Chapter 2 to somebody else's Chapter 15."

It's natural for you to want to be successful, and it's natural for you to want to look as successful as possible RIGHT NOW. Who isn't anxious to reap immediate benefits of being successful in their social environments, such as their work and personal life? But there is a natural progression that must take place during the wealth building process.

In school, you wouldn't expect second graders to read, write, do math, and exhibit critical thinking like that of an eighth grader. Nor would you expect an eighth grader to perform on the same level as the average high school junior. In school, you progress systematically from one grade to another. There is a similar knowledge progression in wealth building.

However, society doesn't label those financial progressions with grade levels for people to compare themselves against. In the real world of personal finance, the grade levels are only known to the individual participants and reflected on their personal net worth statements as financial numbers rather than grade levels. We have to grade ourselves.

Unfortunately, you are not offered learning modules for wealth building during your formal public education. That does not mean that you cannot learn about wealth accumulation or that you cannot continually progress to higher levels during your lifetime. Fortunately, you can continue to learn and acquire more wealth-building skills and knowledge over your entire lifetime. There are no age limits on wealth education.

The reason most people fail financially is that they are prone to skip ahead on their expenditures and rush "the success" part of the process. That's why people buy houses and cars using excessive debt. They are simply rushing to the rewards without earning the goodies through fundamental and robust wealth building. When people don't have the money to buy the goods and services they desire (i.e. by paying cash after they earned the money) they make those emotional purchases by using credit (debt). Banks and corporate lending institutions like credit card companies are well aware of this behavioral trait.

Anybody who is deep in debt didn't start that way. Debt has to start somewhere and through repeated poor decisions, the debt continues to grow until it becomes inescapable.

You will have to come to terms with breaking the process down into smaller steps. Success comes when you focus on just one or two significant objectives at a time.

It's not reasonable (or possible) to learn everything there is on all facets of wealth building, such as investing, or getting promoted at work, or starting a new company, or accounting and benchmarking, all at once in a few short weeks. It is better to master one skill at a time, as opposed to doing a dozen items haphazardly or with poor execution.

A Lot To Learn – One Step At A Time

When you commit to wealth building, you can't successfully implement too many changes at once. The best strategy is to choose one or two goals that you think will move the needle the most. Then focus. Track those items. Benchmark those items. Make notes of those items including what parts of them you can and can't control.

When you first start, there will be some aspects of the journey that you haven't yet mastered. You may not have accurate record keeping. You may not be good at choosing investments. You may not be good at generating more income. You may not be good at being disciplined about saving for an emergency fund.

These are some of the steps, processes, and objectives that you will have to learn and apply as you become a wealth builder. There is nothing worrisome about your lack of natural ability in any area of wealth building. What will make you special and different from everyone else is your ongoing commitment to learning and implementing the necessary skills in the areas that matter in regards to wealth building. But remember, you CAN do it. You can transform your life like many others before you. Sometimes the learning is slow and frustrating. But others have learned and you can too.

There are unlimited opportunities for personal growth and wealth accumulation when you choose to restrict yourself to particular and specific options in your life.

Keep in mind though, when you commit to being a wealth builder, something else will suffer. You can't be all things to all people, nor will you even be the same person anymore. But ultimately that's the point. If you wanted to be the same person, then you would be saying, "I'm fine being broke or not achieving financial success in my lifetime."

This process is about YOU, your results, and your personal transformation.

Don't fool yourself like most others who think that wealth building is a one-time event like a get-rich-quick scheme that looks like this:

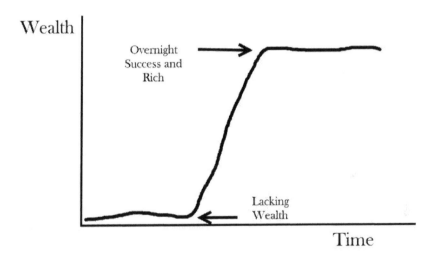

That isn't reality. Breakthrough wealth is a series of constant improvements that evolve as you learn more and apply more skills to your own life. Breakthrough wealth is a series of improvements as you master one phase of your life and move on to higher challenges and accomplishments.

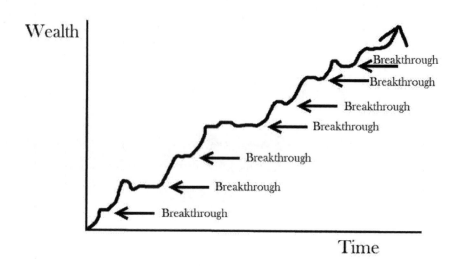

Get Started Now

Most likely you haven't yet put together all the pieces of the wealth puzzle, otherwise you wouldn't be reading this book right now. That is ok. There can be many reasons why you haven't taken the steps to move in a new direction in life. Maybe you just weren't aware that you could be greater? Maybe you didn't have the courage to break away from your peer group or social circles? Maybe your family members kept telling you that accumulating wealth is impossible? That does not matter now.

The Race Against Time

Now, it's only important to focus on the objective of making changes that will impact your future wealth, and it is critical that you get started today. With any financial issue, this statement rings true: TIME IS MONEY.

Everybody has limited time on earth. Everybody has 365 days in a year. Everybody has 24 hours in a day. Wealthy people don't get 26 hours in a day. It doesn't work that way. Wealth builders have the same 24 hours as everybody else. They just choose to use their 24 hours differently than 95+% of the other people on earth.

Time is important on the micro level, which refers to what you do during your days and where you spend your time. It's also important on the macro level, which has to do with how old you are and how much remaining time you have to work with.

The sooner you get started, the more opportunity you will have to build greater wealth.

Think about it this way. Let's pretend that you wanted to be an entrepreneur and start a successful company. Do you know how few people hit a home run the first time they move out of the batter's box and step up to home plate? Life is one giant learning module that never ends. You will never learn everything there is to know about everything.

If you were to start a company for the first time, you would likely make mistakes, solely because of your lack of experience in many areas. You may not know how to manage people, or get products manufactured, or find higher quality or cheaper prices, or track revenues and expenses using an accounting software program. So you would naturally be limited in what you can accomplish until you progress through knowledge and experience to a higher level.

Progressing to higher levels in life requires time to accomplish. Successful entrepreneurs often fail multiple times. Or as they say, "It took me fifteen years to become an overnight success." The sooner you start, the more time you will have to progress to higher levels in your life.

Get started NOW. You will thank yourself later. Or conversely, if you don't start, and you continue to dilly-dally, I can tell you what you will eventually have later in life - and perhaps you already have a good dose of this – REGRET. Don't live a life of regret. Get started now and start learning and making progress on your individual wealth building goals and objectives.

Do Your Best

Life is hard. I want to share some insight with you. Life is hard for everybody. Life is hard at both ends of the social spectrum. Sure, people at the lower end of the social spectrum will say, "Yeah, but my life is harder because I don't have a lot of nice material items in my life." And that would be true. Their life is hard and will continue to be hard.

But even those who have progressed have a hard life because they are making a lot of sacrifices along the way. They are living with deferred gratification. They are living with deferred consumption. They are living with restraint. They are working very hard and giving up their free time in pursuit of individual financial goals. Constantly working hard and diligently is very hard to do, and that is exactly why the majority of people don't do it. Doing nothing is the easiest route to take in life. The harder path is the one filled with work.

So, Why Aren't They Climbing?

Such a paradox leads to an interesting juncture in society because those at the lower end of the social scale will say, "But it's not as hard for those other people who have more." But if it is easier higher up the social ladder, why aren't they doing the things necessary to climb it? Why aren't others using their free time to read books, work overtime, start companies, handle potential failures, and even lose money while learning the skills? Why aren't others trading their personal time for self-education? Why don't they strive for good grades in school? Why? They don't do those things and exhibit those behaviors because all of those endeavors are HARD! That is the only reason why people don't do them.

It will be hard no matter the route you take in life. If you want to be a wealth builder, your life will be hard. If you don't want to be a wealth builder, your life will of course, still be hard. Choose wisely and consciously.

No One Said It Would Be Easy

If you are committing to a life of wealth building, then I encourage you to do your best. When you do your best, you won't live a life of regret.

Be aware that doing your best is a variable endeavor. None of us ever perform at maximum potential every second of every day. Sometimes you will get tired. Sometimes you will get frustrated. Sometimes you will get discouraged. Sometimes you will get distracted. Sometimes you will get sick. Sometimes somebody you love will need help.

In those circumstances, still do your best. Be honest and ask yourself, "Am I doing my best right now with my current situation?"

Trying your best and then being patient with yourself when you aren't performing to maximum capacity may sound contradicting. Many factors in life seem contradicting and paradoxical. However, life is not all about suffering. The purpose of life is not to strip all joy out of your existence. That is a wasted life.

Wealth building is a choice. The reason you make that choice is to be happier overall. You make that commitment and choice because you believe your life will be better overall as a wealth builder than your life would be as a non-wealth builder. You make decisions, sacrifices, and trade-offs that improve the totality of your life, not diminish your overall existence.

Wealth allows you freedom over your time. Wealth allows you access to top medical and healthcare services. Wealth allows you to eat quality foods. Wealth allows you to obtain goods and services that are luxury items. Wealth allows you to have experiences that you couldn't have without the financial resources, like travel and time off.

The pursuit of wealth is a choice that is made to improve your life, not to destroy your life and sometimes there will be a fine line that you must not cross. There are countless people on this earth who work extremely hard seven days a week. They suffer as they work. They suffer with their personal relationships. They suffer as they progress through life. If you find yourself in a situation where most of your life involves suffering, then you are failing in life, and it's time to regroup and assess what is going wrong.

To do your best means putting in the time, the effort, and the energy into pursuits that are most meaningful to you. Happiness results when you make progress towards goals and objectives that are important to you. When you are moving towards goals that you want, your happiness will flourish. When you are moving away from goals that you value, your happiness is fleeting.

You have a right to be happy in life. You will find success in the pursuit of happiness when you do your best on the items that are most important to you.

Remember that a wealth building lifestyle is something that should enhance your life and make you happier. You aren't doing this as personal punishment. Life isn't a contest on who can suffer and deny themselves the most. That isn't the goal. Wealth building allows you to build and spend MORE money, not less. It's just that few people realize this because they never accomplish a wealth standard of existence so that they can experience the benefits first hand.

Observe And Learn From Others

There is a saying that, "You are a reflection of the people who surround you the most." Humans are social creatures who are influenced by one another. If you are a parent, you know this to be true. If your kid is generally well behaved, but starts hanging around a bunch of hooligans, is it more likely that your good kid will change the others or that the others will have a negative influence on your child?

Positive Role Models Will Pave The Way

This social dynamic continues as you progress through life. You are influenced by those who surround you. Thus, it is imperative that you start to seek out, observe, and learn from others whom you want to emulate.

If you want to be healthy, surround yourself with people who have behaviors you admire. Observe them. What do they eat? What do they read? What do they do for fun? How do they structure their day? When do they go to bed? How do they fit in exercise or physical activities during their day?

The same is true for wealth building. If you want to be wealthy, seek out and observe other wealthy people. Seeking out and surrounding yourself with other wealthy individuals may be difficult to do in the beginning when you may not have access to such people. You may have to bridge the initial gap with books, podcasts, learning courses, and online forums. But it can be done.

The internet has been a wonderful tool to connect like-minded people with one another. There are many blogs, forums, and social communities where you can meet and interact with like-minded people. You can follow my blog and lessons at **www.paulkindzia.com**

You will gain comfort and confidence when you learn what others are doing or what they did to achieve what you want to achieve for yourself. You will learn tips and ideas to incorporate into your personal life.

If you want to run a marathon, it helps when you talk to others who have already run a marathon. How did they train? What did they eat for energy? How many miles did they run each week? What did they learn? What mistakes did they make? What training tools did they find useful? How nervous and uncertain were they in their training leading up to their first marathon race?

You want to take a similar approach to wealth building. In marathon running, newer athletes often seek out and hire a coach to help them through the process. That is very efficient because you are obtaining one-on-one individualized advice. It is similar to a wealth builder seeking out a qualified and credentialed wealth advisor or financial planner, not just a sales person looking to earn a commission by selling you a financial product.

Others will seek out experienced runners in running groups or through the local running store to provide guidance based on their many years of experience. People are willing to help others succeed when you show them that you are serious about learning and are willing to do the work necessary for achievement.

If you want to build wealth, it helps to talk to others who have already built wealth. What did they do? What did they learn? What mistakes did they make? (Trust me, they made plenty of mistakes along the way.) What tools did they find useful? How uncertain were they along the way at different points of progress?

"It's hard to soar like an eagle when you are hanging out with a bunch of turkeys all day."

Help Others

It is difficult to succeed without the help of others. Others before us have taken the time to write articles, write books, create tools, share wisdom, pass on mistakes, and carve a smoother path through thick forests of unproductivity.

We learn both from our first-hand experiences where you try techniques for yourself, and through the experiences of others who have come before you. There are plenty of successful individuals who have already figured out the process of wealth building and are willing to pass on their knowledge to those interested in learning.

You must remember that no matter where you are in your journey, there are others who are already many levels above you. Likewise, regardless of how little you are starting out with, there will be others who will still be many levels below you. You can obtain not only knowledge but encouragement, coaching, mentoring, and a helping hand from others who share common goals and pursuits.

You may think to yourself, "I can't help anybody because I don't know much or haven't yet accomplished much." But that is not true. The fact that you are seeking wisdom as you take steps towards improvement and start to implement new resources and ideas means that you are many steps ahead of others who are further back or stuck entirely.

You may worry what others will think if you make changes to your life. You may fear that they will resent you or question you or make fun of you. But on the other hand, you might have the power to inspire them. They may also desire a change. They may also be seeking knowledge and self-improvement. If that is the case, be sure to help others.

"When you learn, teach. When you get, give." – Maya Angelou

"While we teach, we learn." – Seneca

You are similar to those who surround you which means that most of the people with whom you associate are probably around the same level of wealth as you are, and probably all striving to have more and show more success, just like you. You are likely very similar to others in your neighborhood and community. It is very unusual to have households with $2 million homes intermixed with households with $150,000 homes.

Be sensitive to the fact that not everybody wants the same changes as you, nor are they on the same time frame as you. You have your individual path to follow. Forcing your newfound knowledge on others is not the desired intent of this exercise. Rather, it is to become aware that others around you might also be in search of positive personal changes regarding finances, and it can be quite effective to work together in pursuit of common goals.

It's similar to the desire to get in better physical shape. Is it easier or harder when others around you are doing it together? Is it easier or harder when someone else is holding you accountable to your goals and achievements? Is it easier or harder when multiple people are in it together and sharing knowledge, experience, and feedback as to what is and isn't working?

If you wanted to improve your health, you would most likely find it is easier to meet a new friend who has similar goals as you do at a gym rather than at a local bar on a Wednesday night. Choose your hang out spots and social surroundings appropriately based on your desires and goals in life.

There is not a shortage of people who desire an improvement in their personal finances. Most would love to be in a position to build wealth at a faster pace, or even just begin to build real wealth. Reach out and help others who can use a helping hand, words of encouragement, and empathy as they make mistakes, and also help them celebrate their breakthroughs.

You will get more out of it than you can imagine.

Accumulate For Real

There's a difference between reading about wealth building and practicing a wealth-building lifestyle. There is no substitute for the actual performance of the behaviors and habits of a wealth builder. There's a difference between thinking about wealth accumulation casually in your free time and when you feel like it and building wealth because it's your job, your mission, and your goal.

A Focused Effort

Many people read and hear about different approaches to personal finances over their lifetime. They might clip a coupon, shop a sale, or throw in a resume for a job opportunity a level above them, but they never take the plunge and consistently do what is necessary for long-term success.

Lack of action is a form of financial self-sabotage. It's like sands through the hourglass, with time slipping away with each grain that falls with gravity.

You should not be afraid of certain challenges that need to be overcome to reach your goal. It may be fear of rejection. It may be fear of failure. It may be fear of change. It may be fear of social ridicule – which is interesting when you think how some people will criticize you for improving yourself financially while most people want to improve *themselves* financially.

Here's the truth about wealth building: Until you start accumulating financial resources, it doesn't matter. The proof is in the accumulation.

If you aren't committed to increasing income, decreasing expenses, saving money, eliminating debt, and investing wisely, nothing is going to work. I don't care how many books you've read or how many wealthy people you have come across or dream about imitating.   You need to start accumulating capital, and that will only happen when you increase income and reduce spending. Nobody is going to do that part for you.

If you can't accumulate capital – even if you start with small amounts in the beginning – nothing else is going to come together. No financial freedom. No control over your time. No emergency fund. NOTHING. NADA. ZIPPO.

You may have dreams. Dreams are nice. You may have intentions.   Intentions are nice. You may have potential. Potential is nice. But if you never start accumulating capital, nothing is going to happen.

"A penny saved is a penny earned."

"Slow and steady fills the purse."

If you don't like the slow approach, take a faster approach. Earn more money. Read books on the subject. Invest in a weekend workshop or online courses.   Expand your knowledge in each of the key areas of wealth building. There are people who have figured out how to make every level of income imaginable, from $10,000 a year to millions and millions a year. Somebody has already figured it out and was willing to do what it took to make it happen.

Wealth building is a good, honest endeavor. You only have a limited amount of time to achieve it while accomplishing other life goals. You can spend time thinking about wealth building, or you can spend the necessary time doing it. The more time you spend thinking about it and not doing it is reducing your potential since time is passing.

Give yourself some deadlines and make them concrete. When are you going to be done with debt? When are you going to accumulate your first $100,000? When will you have your first $1,000,000?

Every wealth builder has had to overcome the paralysis of inaction and fear. You are not unique and certainly not alone with those feelings. Every wealth builder started somewhere. They had to start just like you. Wherever you are on your journey, thousands have had to progress through that point, and just like you will have to progress to a higher level. They did it, and you can do it too.

There are always higher levels to achieve, new skills to learn, and new techniques to acquire. Start with those that most apply to your situation. Move your wealth up. Accumulate capital. You must accumulate.

If you find yourself at the end of the month at the same place you started at the beginning of the month, you must acknowledge a need to change. If you find yourself at the end of the year at the same place you did at the start of the year, you must acknowledge a need to change. You must accumulate if you are to be a successful wealth builder. Learning how to accumulate and bust through plateaus leads to breakthrough wealth and climbing to higher levels of achievement.

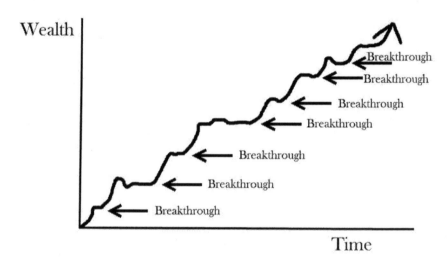

You Can Make Two Mistakes With Savings

Have you ever wondered how much you should be saving each week, month, or year? The "how much should I be saving?" question is a very commonly asked one. Let me share a perspective on this topic. Many individuals get so wrapped up in the intricacies of formulas and math that they forget about the big picture goals of wealth building.

If you ever find yourself getting wrapped up in the minutia of the math and formulas in regards to your savings, I offer you the following that I call, "The two mistakes with savings."

Mistake #1 – Saving too little

Mistake #2 – Saving too much

Mistake #1 – Saving Too Little
Let's go through some scenarios if you make this mistake and save too little during your life.

- We all age. When you get older, you lose energy. You can't work the way you used to. A reduction in work output will either be due to your lack of energy and physical abilities or due to employers not wanting to hire old farts to staff their businesses, usually because they can't perform as well as younger and cheaper employees.

- Your earned income diminishes. You can't make what you used to especially if you had a job that required physical output to perform.
- Your technology skills diminish when compared to younger workers who tend to be more technologically savvy.
- You still have all of your normal expenses that you did before you aged and you may even have additional ones like more healthcare needs.

When people find themselves later in life without adequate financial resources, it stinks because they lost the ability to correct the deficits or do much about it. Necessary and desired financial goals should already be completed. If not, those that are under-saved are left in quite a bind that will be permanent as they progress and ride into the sunset of their life.

When you think about it, if you save too little, you get to a point in life where there is little that you can do to correct the error of your ways. You backed yourself into a corner with no options out. That doesn't sound like fun does it?

Unfortunately, I have had seen plenty of these situations in my days as a financial advisor. Many people at this point seek out a financial advisor at that "oh-crap" moment when they are desperate. They ask with desperation and pleading, "Tell me what to do to correct this terrible problem that I find myself in." The only reasonable replies are:

1. "I would panic."
2. "Build a time machine and travel backwards."

Note that neither response goes over very well. You aren't allowed to say those types of things in client meetings with terrified people.

Do not wait until you have to correct a major financial problem. An ounce of prevention is worth a pound of cure. You need to think about your future and prepare for those days ahead of time.

Wealth problems can be similar to marriage. You should not wait to call a marriage counselor when your spouse hands you divorce papers.

Mistake #2 – Saving Too Much

What about that dreaded Mistake #2 where you have saved too much money? Here is the most common scenario I see:

- If you wake up one day and are like, "I have this terrible problem, and I don't know what to do about it. I have TOO MUCH MONEY!"

A problem like this is different from Mistake #1 because this problem has an easy solution. If you ever find yourself with far too much money and don't know what to do about it, please call or email me immediately. I have a solution for this.

I keep extra-large crowbars in my office for just such an emergency. If you cannot open up your wallet and let some of that money explode out of there, I have special tools and programs to help you find ways to spend your savings. You can fix such a problem. It does cause a little discomfort because you aren't used to these corrective measures, but rest assured there are solutions to your "I have too much money" problem, and I can help you!

The Iron Law Of Investing

As you develop your wealth-building skills, you undoubtedly will have to enter the world of investing. Investing is by no means limited to the stock market. Although many people use the stock market as a primary method of building and preserving wealth, it is by no means the only path to wealth.

Whether you plan on investing in the stock market or investing in other alternatives such as real estate, venture capital, privately owned businesses, or fine art, there is what I call, "The Iron Law Of Investing." The Iron Law of Investing states:

"The price you pay for an investment will greatly influence your eventual rate of return."

If you overpay for any investment that has an expected cash yield, you are essentially locking yourself into subpar returns for an extended period of time. Note that this applies to investing and speculation. *Investing* is buying and holding an asset that is expected to generate a particular yield. *Speculation* is buying an investment or item with the thought that there may be somebody (anybody) else who comes along after the purchase and will pay even more for the item regardless of its underlying intrinsic value.

The Iron Law Of Investing At Work

This Iron Law of Investing applies to all investments that a person can make over a lifetime. Whether you buy a car, house, rental property, business, stock, bond, or oil well, if you overpay for that investment, you are lowering your future expected returns.

People lose sight of this all of the time, especially in bull markets and even worse, during financial bubbles.

Investing comes down to value. Price is what you pay; value is what you get. The questions to ask are, "How much should you be willing to pay now for an asset that should be worth more down the road?" The increase in value down the road and the time that must elapse before it hopefully rises to a higher value will dictate your eventual rate of return.

Imagine you have a neighbor who is getting divorced and needs cash fast. He decides to sell his Honda Accord for $14,000. You are aware of general auto prices and you believe that you could sell the car easily for $18,000. You buy it from the neighbor who needs fast cash for $14,000, and you then sell it at the fair market value a week later for a tidy profit and generate a strong rate of return.

But what if you paid your neighbor $20,000 for the car? The car is the same car as before. Nothing changed about the car. It's a good car. It runs reliably. It's clean and has no dents. It's the same car but with a different buying price. A different buying price will result in a different return on investment. Alas, the "Iron Law of Investing" was alive and well in this example.

The used car example sounds fundamentally simple when you think about it with a Honda Accord in mind. This is an easy example because you can look up used car prices on the internet or through a resource like a used car pricing guide.

But this applies to all potential investments, even those that aren't so easily valued, such houses, stocks, bonds, apartment buildings, storage facilities, gold, or a ship full of iron ore.

Everything has a price and that price will be determined between a willing buyer and seller. If you pay too much for anything, you are reducing your future return potential. If you overpay by too much, you greatly increase the possibilities and probabilities of earning a loss on your investment.

Why Value Matters

As you continue along as a wealth builder, you will have to learn to pay attention to value more and more. You may not be an expert in valuing anything right now. That's ok. Nobody was born a valuation expert. This skill comes from practice and experience. You will have to learn to be proficient in valuing an item rather efficiently if you are to become wealthy.

If you want to invest in stocks, it is certainly going to help to know if you are overpaying or underpaying for a stock based on your intended holding period. Some people want to trade a stock every two seconds while others will want to hold onto a stock for years.

The very best real estate investors will give you the same advice. You make the money when you buy the property, not when you sell. You have to be thinking this concept through at the beginning of any investment.

People become very wealthy when they either solve problems, thus creating a business opportunity, or when they are extremely good at valuing a certain type of asset. They become experts at buying at the right price, managing that asset during an appropriate holding period, and then knowing when it is an opportune time and price to exit the holding.

The purpose of this book is not to get into the technical valuation methods related to any particular investment, which is far beyond the scope of this book. Rather, it is a reminder that the Iron Law of Investing is a concept that you should force yourself to master and abide by throughout your investing career. The better you become at implementing the Iron Law of Investing, the larger and smoother your wealth curve will be.

Risk And Return

Risk and return is a topic that is similar to the Iron Law of Investing. It will sound easy to grasp but is hard to implement when life is happening in real time.

Risk and return should be a reality that makes you give pause before parting with your capital and investing the funds into any investment. Before investing your hard-earned capital, you must stop and ask yourself a few questions;

1. What is my upside potential if I buy an investment at the current price? What is it that I stand to gain? You must progress past the runaway dreams that make you feel as though every investment that you make will go straight to the moon in price right after you invest in it.
2. What is my downside risk? What happens if events don't go as intended? How badly will the worst-case scenario hurt me? It is essential that you brainstorm and consider all the potential reasonable situations of how investments can go wrong or not deliver the desired result.

The Downside To Normal Human Behavior

Now you are probably reading the above guidelines and thinking to yourself, "Those are obvious. Who wouldn't consider those before investing? Unfortunately, the answer is, "Just about everybody at some point in their investing career."

People make completely irrational decisions when it comes to money and investing. When people purchase items that they want, and this even includes items beyond investments, such as cars or houses, they get completely focused on all the wonderful outcomes that they associate with that item – their thoughts, beliefs, and dreams. Focusing on the imagined benefits of ownership is a very common human behavior that leads to errors in judgment.

When people buy a jet ski using a bank loan and a low down payment, they aren't thinking about anything other than being on the lake with their friends and zippidy-do-da-ing on the water in the summer sun. There is no thought to maintenance, insurance, storage, registration fees, monthly payments, or even what purchase will tickle their fancy next month when they are sitting around on a rainy Saturday afternoon when they don't feel like using a jet ski.

One of the largest mistakes that individuals make is in regards to their primary residences. Americans have a fascination with big and expensive homes which usually leads them to buy more than they can really afford. When people shop for a home, they aren't thinking about anything other than their dreams of being in a new house with the kitchen, the family room, the back yard, the finished basement, and closets. They can visualize and imagine themselves in that home so clearly that their purchasing decisions become error prone.

What they don't usually consider when purchasing the home are all of the financial realities that will impact them over the course of owning that home, such as taxes, insurance, increased utilities, repairs and maintenance, and higher mortgage payments.

The same holds true with investments. People rarely give a thought to what can go wrong and how that could impact them. People buy stocks based on "hot tips," invest in a business with their buddies, and borrow money to chase easy money all of the time. Then when events don't go well, it's often a double whammy. Not only did the investment sour, but they bet the farm using borrowed money.

Imagine how people think and feel walking into a Las Vegas casino at the start of an evening. Gamblers focus on the lights, the action, and the potential big wins that they could score, rather than focusing on what could go wrong when they lose, which doesn't seem to occur to them even though the probabilities are stacked against them.

It is imperative that you begin to practice implementing "risk and return" profiles into your investing arsenal of tools. Before making any investment, create a list of what you hope could go right and then spend equal or more time thinking through what could go wrong and how that would impact your life if events don't go as planned. If you spend ample time thinking through the downside scenarios, you will often pass up on many investment opportunities, which is often a very prudent wealth behavior.

It's very difficult to keep growing your wealth and accomplishing breakthroughs if you keep losing it and going backwards. Breakthrough wealth requires consistent forward progress. You will hit obstacles. You will hit plateaus. Learning how to move forward without putting yourself at risk of losing your wealth is important to accomplish breakthroughs.

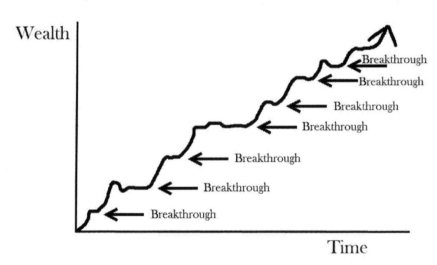

The Risk Paradox

The risk paradox is a behavior seen in investors whereby those who can least afford to take risk, end up taking the most risk. Conversely, those who can most afford to take risk, often end up not taking the risk for fear of losing their hard-earned capital and savings.

Let me provide you with the stories of two different clients and then I want you to select which camp is more appealing.

Couple #1 is Chris and Ann Marie. They are well educated and hard working. They married 15 years ago and are proud parents of two children. They are part of a large group of frustrated and confused investors who can't seem to make the kind of progress that they believe they should be achieving.

Although they live in a very nice house in the suburbs of a large U.S. city, drive nice cars, and send their kids to good schools, they just can't seem to climb the ladder in wealth accumulation.

Their perspective is split between feeling fortunate for what they do have, along with craving for more because they know that they are not on track for a brighter future, like a secure retirement or financial freedom.

They believe that they have identified the problem and have come up with a solution. They believe that the problem is in their investment results. Their solution is to blindly increase the risk in their portfolios, ignoring the Iron Law of Investing and Risk/Return profiles. Their belief is that increasing risk will automatically result in greater returns. After all, you can't make a big score in the markets if you don't take some big risks. It drives stock investors crazy to see certain sectors or areas of the markets moving fast while they only appear to be grinding higher at a moderate pace.

On the surface, it makes a lot of sense. Their desire to be wealthy and reduce worry is tremendous. Their frustrations are equally as powerful. How could it be that they work so hard at their jobs and yet don't seem to be making the kind of forward progress that they expected?

Couple #2 is Frank and Judy. They are at the pinnacle of retirement. After selling their plumbing distribution business that they built over the past 32 years, the couple is thrilled to be reaping the rewards from a lifetime of hard work. Over the course of decades, they saved regularly, invested prudently, and paid off all of their debts.

The sale of the company was a wonderful windfall that was icing on the cake. They enjoy traveling, spending time with the grandchildren, playing golf and tennis, and tackling a major remodeling project in their home.

If the couple had to make mention of a worry, it would be the fear of losing what took them a lifetime to accumulate. They fear financial market risk.

The Paradox At Work

These two varying stories highlight the behavior paradox of investment risk. What wealth advisors often discover is that the investors who are under-accumulated and can least afford financial setbacks are usually tempted to take the MOST risk.

On the other end of the spectrum, investors who accumulate large sums of wealth over long and hard periods of time are usually willing to take the LEAST risk. Their fear is losing what they worked so long and hard to accumulate.

You see this behavioral issue throughout society. Who buys the most lottery tickets (which have terrible odds of success), the wealthy or the poor? Who do you expect to find at the casino slot machines hoping for their financial problems to be solved, the wealthy or the poor?

It does make sense from an emotional and behavioral perspective. If someone feels hopeless and frustrated in life and hasn't figured out how "inputs" equal "outputs" over long periods of time, what else can they do other than to take long shots? They lack the skills, experience, and wisdom of the alternative yet proven path to increased wealth.

"A fool and his money are always separated." – Unknown

Some Things Never Change

Financial markets will always go through cycles because they are made up of humans transacting with one another. Humans are flawed and core human behaviors will never change (or at least in our lifetimes). Most humans are not naturally wired for investing success. Humans are emotional and social creatures who take comfort in being a part of the greater community.

It's natural to seek out what appears to be the path of least resistance. And there are certainly benefits. It can make you more efficient and effective and optimize your time as you model yourself off of others who have the success that you desire.

The Problem With Greed

Unfortunately, most investors model themselves off of the wrong financial behaviors. More often than not, people tend to mimic the unwise spending patterns of the non-wealthy rather than the investing and behavioral patterns of proven wealth builders.

We are programmed to become attracted to what is most appealing in the short run and provide immediate gratification. This behavior allows humans to get caught up in euphoria and emotions that often result in poor investing or financial decisions. If it appears that there is "easy money to be made," who doesn't want a piece of that action?

It doesn't matter if it is a hot stock tip from your crazy uncle or word that real estate values are rocketing in the Florida Panhandle where you could buy a pre-construction condo with no money down. Get rich quick schemes will always be effective at attracting attention because get rich quick schemes take advantage of behavioral flaws in the human system.

Markets go in cycles because humans are perpetually swinging from episodes of greed to fear to greed and back to fear again.

These ebbs and flows of markets can often cause bubbles of spectacular magnitude. Of course, once the dust settles and the majority of people lose their money, everyone can look back and say, "What were we thinking?" But try asking that when it appears that there is easy money to be made either in real estate, stocks, oil, gold, or any investment fad that takes valuations to unfathomable levels.

Greed is a very powerful human behavior, and it will trump patience and logic at the most inopportune times. To become a successful investor, you must learn to control your emotions. In particular, be aware of emotions that deal with greed and fear and your desire to follow the crowds.

Starting Over

Sometimes our biggest fear in life is starting over. This fear could relate to a big issue, or a smaller issue. However, starting over could also be a wonderful opportunity. If you tried something and it didn't work, then you must simply start over with another approach that may work more effectively.

"Insanity is doing the same thing over and over again and expecting different results." – Albert Einstein

It is time to progress to the next level. It may be long overdue in your life. It is time to give up on your ideals of perfection and a lucky winning lottery ticket to success. The path won't be a perfect one. It will be bumpy and rocky. It will have twists and turns.

Wealth building will not be easy. Everything inside of you will be tempted to wait to get started or make the necessary changes tomorrow, next week, or next year. Your inner self will naturally want to procrastinate. Taking action and moving forward with new processes is what you must do if you want to be successful and build wealth.

If you feel nervous and unsure, that is natural. You are experiencing normal emotions. You must take a leap of faith and commitment. Have faith that you will create a better life for yourself and move past your current levels. But you must also have the commitment to make that faith a reality. Trust in yourself that you can make changes one step at a time, which will lead to forward progress towards your wealth goals and objectives.

When you learn and implement the required changes in your life, you will begin to get the results and transformation that you seek. You will slowly become a different person.

But you must not wait. Take action, do your best, accumulate capital, and progress to the next level. Find the courage to push yourself out of your current state and level. Once you stop dreaming and start doing, your life will have a fascinating way of falling into place as you get results and experience a transformation.

YOU CAN DO IT

OTHERS HAVE PROVEN IT COULD BE DONE

MAKE YOUR MARK ON THE WORLD

LIVE IN PURSUIT OF YOUR GOALS

What's Next?

This is the part of the story where you have to figure out for yourself what is next for you. What goals have you selected for yourself? Are you at step number one of the wealth building process and just deciding to make the leap into becoming a permanent wealth builder for life? Or are you a few more steps into the process but stuck on a plateau for a prolonged period of time and not progressing as fast as you would like?

Breakthrough wealth is a continuous process of achievement. I would love to continue helping you along your path to wealth and reaching new heights. We are here to teach you how to improve your life through personal financial management.

You can tell me what you thought and share it with your friends by visiting us at **www.paulkindzia.com**

About The Author

Paul Kindzia is a writer, portfolio manager, wealth advisor, and CEO of Kindzia Investments, Inc. a registered investment advisory practice outside of Atlanta, GA. His personal mission is to teach others how to improve their lives through the process of personal financial management.

Paul has over 25 years of experience working in the accounting and financial services industry.

He started his career as a CPA and consultant at the international firm Ernst & Young, LLP where he worked in both the Atlanta, GA office and in the national headquarters office which was in Cleveland, OH at the time.

With a desire to work with individual clients rather than corporate entities, he left the corporate world and became the original founder of Niagara Financial Advisors, LLC an SEC registered investment advisory firm in Alpharetta, GA.

With a goal of teaching and assisting clients to achieve a wealthy, healthy, and happy lifestyle that is geared towards meaning and personal fulfillment, he then founded Kindzia Investments, Inc.

Paul is a certified public accountant with an undergraduate degree from the State University of New York at Buffalo (1992). He also holds an MBA in corporate finance from the State

University of New York at Buffalo (1994). He is a member of the American Institute of Certified Public Accountants.

Paul is a Certified Financial Planner (CFP®).

He is an avid reader and writer with an ever expanding personal library. He has a love of nature, science, animals, and the ocean.

Paul is a proponent of maintaining personal health and wellness. He enjoys an active and healthy lifestyle and is a 13-time Ironman triathlon finisher. He has also completed numerous marathons including but not limited to the San Diego Rock N' Roll Marathon, Nashville Country Music Marathon, Disney Marathon, New York City Marathon, and his personal favorite the Marine Corp Marathon in Washington, D.C.

Paul lives outside of Atlanta, GA with his family and an ever-expanding pack of rescue dogs. He is an animal lover at heart and the family often volunteers with English Springer Rescue America (ESRA) or helping out some stray cats.

He also enjoys behavioral finance, investments, endurance athletics, martial arts, music, video production, making sushi and has a tremendous passion for fishing and scuba diving.

You can keep up with him at **www.paulkindzia.com**

For additional valuable information including free resources, please visit our website at:

www.paulkindzia.com

Most people never build adequate wealth which leads to daily stress. We teach proven financial processes based on timeless principles that results in happier, more fulfilling, and balanced lives.

51216111R00109

Made in the USA
Columbia, SC
15 February 2019